QUEERLY CENTERED

QUEERLY CENTERED

LGBTQA Writing Center Directors Navigate the Workplace

TRAVIS WEBSTER

UTAH STATE UNIVERSITY PRESS
Logan

© 2021 by University Press of Colorado

Published by Utah State University Press
An imprint of University Press of Colorado
245 Century Circle, Suite 202
Louisville, Colorado 80027

 The University Press of Colorado is a proud member of
the Association of University Presses.

The University Press of Colorado is a cooperative publishing enterprise supported,
in part, by Adams State University, Colorado State University, Fort Lewis College,
Metropolitan State University of Denver, Regis University, University of Alaska Fairbanks,
University of Colorado, University of Denver, University of Northern Colorado,
University of Wyoming, Utah State University, and Western Colorado University.

∞ This paper meets the requirements of the ANSI/NISO Z39.48–1992 (Permanence of
Paper)

ISBN: 978-1-64642-148-0 (paperback)
ISBN: 978-1-64642-149-7 (ebook)
https://doi.org/10.7330/9781646421497

Library of Congress Cataloging-in-Publication Data

Names: Webster, Travis, author.
Title: Queerly centered : LGBTQA writing center directors navigate the workplace /
   Travis Webster.
Description: Logan : Utah State University Press, [2021] | Includes bibliographical refer-
   ences and index.
Identifiers: LCCN 2021029476 (print) | LCCN 2021029477 (ebook) | ISBN
   9781646421480 (paperback) | ISBN 9781646421497 (ebook)
Subjects: LCSH: Writing centers—Administration. | English language—Rhetoric—Study
   and teaching (Higher) | Sexual minorities in higher education.
Classification: LCC PE1404 .W43 2021 (print) | LCC PE1404 (ebook) | DDC
   808/.0420711—dc23
LC record available at https://lccn.loc.gov/2021029476
LC ebook record available at https://lccn.loc.gov/2021029477

The University Press of Colorado gratefully acknowledges the support provided by
Virginia Tech University toward the support of this publication.

Cover illustration by EgudinKa/Shutterstock.

For Gary, for my parents, and for twenty fabulous participants who helped me learn even more about the quite queer world of writing center administration and LGBTQA identity.

CONTENTS

ACKNOWLEDGMENTS

I first thank the Utah State University Press acquisitions editor, Rachael Levay. I can't imagine this journey without her unflagging support, tireless mentorship, and queer allyship. I owe gratitude to Michael Spooner, who listened to my first, very green query just before his retirement, supportively transferring my proposal to Rachael when she took over as editor. I extend gracious thank-yous to the anonymous reviewers for their generous, directive feedback in making the project much better than it would have been. Many thanks to Utah State University Press across the board for an amazing first book experience, including the support of Kami Day, Laura Furney, Dan Pratt, Darrin Pratt, and Beth Svinarich.

I appreciate the support of the International Writing Centers Association—for a generous research grant, for a generative 2016 Summer Institute, and for its LGBTQA Standing Group, especially Trixie Smith and Jay Sloan. I thank Pace University, the Dyson College of Arts and Sciences, and the provost's office for research release and travel funding, and offer gratitude to my colleagues in the English and Modern Language Studies Department and beyond, including Meaghan Brewer, Dana Cadman, Maureen Colgan, Jane Collins, Bette Kirschstein, Ann Marie McGlynn, Vyshali Manivannan, Kate Mulhollem, Rob Mundy, Ama Wattley, and Adelia Williams. Thanks to the amazing staff, especially Jason, at the Barnes and Noble Café in Lake Mohegan, New York, where I wrote most of this book.

From my University of Houston–Clear Lake Writing Center family, I appreciate the inspiration and support of Adrian Russell, Conor Bracken, Kelly Keefe, Martin Giron, Jay Hernandez, Austin Green, Lourdes Zavaleta, Ryan Smith, and Christal Seahorn. Colleague-friends Matt Cox, Laurie McMillan, Anna Sicari, Jessica Restaino, Jackie Grutsch McKinney, Beth Boquet, Timothy Oleksiak, Zack Turpin, Randall Monty, Beth Towle, and Mark Hall deserve special thanks for their encouragement. Early mentors will always deserve special gratitude, especially Michele Simmons, Jim Zebroski, Paul Butler, Will Banks, Mike Martin, Norjuan Austin, and Kimberly Wristers O'Malley.

I hope to pay forward the gift of Michele Eodice's mentorship one day, which I am deeply thankful for. It was Michele who first encouraged me to query Utah State University Press and facilitated my first meeting with Michael Spooner. She also regularly supported my writing process during her fantastic online retreats.

Hadi Banat is a dear friend I met at this project's finale. I cherish his care, calm, and new-but-familiar friendship. He deserves special thanks for helping me with the book title and listening and offering feedback as I made final revisions.

Thanks go to my Miami University family. Jonathan Rylander, my coauthor on another project, kept me focused, calm, and supported during this one. Chanon Adsanatham and Bre Garrett were a generous and loving support system through our ongoing online message thread about work, writing, and scholarship. Lisa Blankenship's generous feedback and Caroline Dadas's loving encouragement were critical as I submitted this book's first draft. I will always associate submitting that draft with the joy of later hosting their wedding.

Michelle Miley's support and humor has been with me since we overlapped for a few short weeks at the University of Houston in the summer of 2013; we stayed in contact and have become dear friends and colleagues. She was the first to suggest I showcase this book's unicorn conversation with a participant, and she offered insightful feedback on this book's earliest drafts for which I am ever grateful.

Harry Denny has helped me with this project more times than I can count, never once complaining, only ever offering a listening ear and nudges of regular encouragement and occasional tough love. I talked, texted, and Zoomed with him about this book for years, day and night. I thank him for his patience and generosity, and for *The Devil Wears Prada* memes and hound pictures that kept me going during every stage of this process.

Rebecca Hallman Martini has been with me since this project was a few poorly articulated ideas rolling around in my head. Together, over four years, we Skyped weekly, wrote sole-authored books side by side, and saw each other through the ups and downs of the job market, of the tenure track, of publishing, and of academia. She helped me more on this project than I could ever properly thank her for.

I extend thanks to my family of Earth and Heaven, including Websters, Gammages, Larsons, Vanderveers, Pembrokes, Borsellinos, Winklers,

Gainouses, Barmores, Dodgens, Russells, Simonette-Kirklands, Antosca-DiGangis, Novaks, and Lancasters; to my parents' spouses, Kleta and Robin; and to my oldest friend of twenty years, Nicole.

Forever and always, I thank my parents, Rusty and Belynda. Each time I reach a professional milestone, I realize they were with me all along, as is said in *The Wizard of Oz*. In the case of this book, their early advice to listen to people, to learn and, to try to do good in the world was front and center. Academia has taken me away from them geographically, though I always keep close to my heart A. A. Milne's words of wisdom about love, distance, and being apart, which they both know well.

I send loving thanks to my husband Gary Larson and our dachshund-poodle mix, Betty, who deserve this book's most notable recognition for showing love, support, kindness, and patience during the years-long writing process. Gary, honey, to answer your question from about three years ago, yes, the book's finally done. This milestone has been a long time coming, and you've been with me every step, helping me believe in and amplify myself, despite many professional setbacks. Thanks especially for encouraging me to "call them back." I couldn't have known my entire professional life would forever change for the better with those three words of wisdom. As I have since 2012, I remember that "this must be the place." I love you, forever and always.

I close feeling fortunate to have had the chance to talk with and learn from a fabulous group of queer writing center practitioners. They taught me more about the work of writing centers and queer leadership than I could have ever imagined or properly thank them for. They are this book, and I'm grateful for their trust in me to write it.

Short selections from this book also appear in volume 39, issues 1 and 2, of *The Writing Center Journal*, with permissions from both publication venues.

QUEERLY CENTERED

1

INTRODUCTION

In the early-morning hours of June 12, 2016, a terrorist entered Orlando's gay club, *Pulse*, on Latin Night and opened fire, murdering forty-nine people, injuring another fifty-three. Just before news of the shooting broke, I lay awake in a hotel room, energized, following an intensive week at that year's International Writing Centers Association Summer Institute (IWCA SI). In bed, I scrolled social media, my blood pressure rising and my mouth drying, as the earliest *Pulse* coverage surfaced in my newsfeed. I didn't sleep that night, haunted by young, queer people dying; most were people of color and from working-class backgrounds who went out just to dance in a supposed queer[1] safe space. By morning, as I packed to leave IWCA SI, I saw coverage of Eddie Jamoldroy Justice. Trapped in a *Pulse* bathroom, he texted his mother, Mina Justice, for an hour, pleading for her help and saying his goodbyes (Park 2016). Within an hour, his life went from enjoying himself at a historic gay venue to barricading himself in a bathroom with other victims, awaiting the inevitable. He stuck with me. I thought of my earlier life of going out, dancing, drinking, and enjoying gay life. I thought of queer friends of my youth, our community of 1990s gay culture. With IWCA SI fresh on my mind, I thought of my tutors, many of whom reminded me of the victims—their faces, their backgrounds, their dreams in the making.

I returned to work Monday in the writing center feeling punched in the stomach, afraid, and angry. I didn't want to talk about the events, didn't yet know how to. John, a participant in this book, who is an Orlando writing center director,[2] would later teach me much about articulating my complicated feelings about the *Pulse* murders. In his interview, he told me he was quite jarred by these events, which were local to his center. He struggled with the shooting but felt *Pulse*, an atrocity that impacted mostly queer, transgender, and working-class people of color, wasn't his tragedy to mourn as a privileged white gay man—a sentiment I identified with and struggle with even now. His tutors, many of whom were queer people of color who knew or knew of *Pulse* victims, contested his personal tensions. Together, he and his tutors held a writing event in

DOI: 10.7330/9781646421497.c001

the center to help the university community cope with grief and fear, as this book's later chapters showcase. The event was critical since students at his university looked to the writing center for solace, he says, arising naturally from the intimate, one-to-one nature of writing center work. He told me then that his queer identity made him more open to such work in the first place—a theme that surfaces often in this study.

Like John, I first struggled with talking about *Pulse* with my writing center staff—what to say, what to do, whether I was the person to do this work. At first I said nothing. I was stung, distracted, paralyzed by Eddie's story and the stories of others fallen and injured. I was haunted by Texas's then-recently passed conceal-carry legislation for state universities, which would go into effect by fall 2016, whereby people could legally bring guns, concealed, onto state university campuses. Late in the day, a few tutors, queer and nonqueer alike, dropped by my office seeking community and support, asking for guidance about their own fears concerning the murders. I listened and I consoled while scared and exhausted myself, even in my privileged position and body. A senior tutor—a straight white woman in her fifties—encouraged me to write the staff and the broader community, saying I was the person to do so, referring to my out gay director identity. She said the staff needed me to write. I did. To this day, it remains the most difficult professional correspondence I've ever produced.[3]

In my memo to my staff, I offered my office for *Pulse* conversations for anyone who needed support. In my office, I heard fear and anger. I heard anxiety about similar events happening at our university—a Hispanic-serving institution on the cusp of conceal-carry legislation in a conservative state. My tutors feared similar events could take place specifically at our center given our very "out" social justice mission and our staff made up of many queer people and queer people of color. This work was somewhere between profoundly rewarding and deeply uncomfortable. I felt equipped for (as participant John alludes to) and called to do this work, like many other queer writing center administrators, which is to say that as a queer writing center director, I wasn't alone. I noticed through disciplinary venues, such as the WCenter Listserv and IWCA social media, that it was most often queer practitioners who labored to help others make sense of the tragedies through writing center outreach. I noticed and heard through private and public conversations that queer directors had complicated feelings about this work, understanding the labor as critically necessary and deeply embodied but emotionally trying and occasionally exhausting.

I start with this story because, from that memory alone, this project will always be hauntingly enmeshed in how I think about my work as a queer writing center director. This book is about queer people and queer work, but stories like these speak to us all in the discipline, regardless of our orientations. I say this not only because we are empathetic and compassionate about tragedies upon queer bodies but also because these events that impact bodies shape our work—as administrative leaders, as disciplinary professionals, and as people—in writing centers beyond the work of tutoring. *Pulse* led me to think about my queer body and my administration, especially the ways queer writing center labor intersects with national issues that impact people of difference. But *Pulse* also led me to inquire deeply, personally, into queer leadership in the writing center field, alongside but also far beyond the work of peer writing tutoring. My orientations to queer writing center research and attention to these events make this book what it is: a study of what queer writing center directors say about their administrative labor; a study about their labor's implications for what we, in the writing center field, talk about when we talk about writing center administration; and a discussion of how, because it's through a queer lens, this study aligns and departs from current conversations about writing center administrative labor.

FORWARD DIRECTIONS

Following the *Pulse* murders and their impact on my center and tutors, I have sought to understand relationships between queer identities and administrative posts, especially the evoked work that takes place when queer people take on writing center directorships, as well as the disciplinary implications of that work alongside and beyond lore and hearsay. However, lore and hearsay are quite loud in the broader discipline: for example, in a conversation at a recent International Writing Centers Association (IWCA) Conference, two other queer writing center directors and I spoke about our work lives. Just that week, I had helped a transgender tutor navigate their coming-out process to other tutors and had felt pushback during a staff meeting in which I noted writing centers could house social justice missions. My comments sparked head nods from both colleagues. One had just been asked to serve on a campus-climate committee to offer a queer voice. Another colleague, having recently left one administrative post for another, confided how being bullied at his previous institution—namely being called homophobic slurs—impacted his ability to lead his center and support his tutors; being bullied and responding to such treatment, he said, was its own kind of work. In wrapping up our conversation, we noted that queer-led writing centers signal distinct labor and commented, somewhat in jest, that many nonqueer writing center colleagues often disregard such claims as mere lore, countering and drowning queer stories with their own less relevant straight ones. At the same conference, I heard similar sentiments to my colleagues' and mine echoed at the special interest group for LGBTQA writing center practitioners.

In this sense, *Queerly Centered: LGBTQA Writing Center Directors Navigate the Workplace* speaks to writing center administrative labor and queer identity at a key moment in Western culture's history in which queer people face concurrent progression, regression, oppression, and violence (as articulated in the previous and next section), and whereby attention to and equity and access for minorities at work is critical. Such a book is kairotic given that writing center research seeks to examine the realities of its work and workers alongside a complicated queer local and global zeitgeist—one relatively absent from book-length writing center studies.

To echo Nicole Caswell, Jackie Grutsch McKinney, and Rebecca Jackson (2016) in *The Working Lives of New Writing Center Directors*, this study is "about a job" (3) but specifically examines what labor looks like when queer people direct writing centers, especially what local and disciplinary phenomena surface alongside queer writing center leadership. This framework informs *Queerly Centered*'s central research questions, grounded in interviews with twenty queer writing center directors: What makes up the labor and lived, on-the-job experiences of these writing center administrators? What might accounts and analyses of such queer labor teach writing center administrators about writing center work, especially as it interplays with capital, activism, and tension on the job?

Such questions give way to how these twenty queer writing center practitioners teach us, as a discipline, about administrative labor. Participants' work showcases nuanced, complex labors not yet acknowledged, documented, or investigated formally in the writing center field's research. Queer labor is linked (1) to participants' queer backgrounds (what chapter 2 calls *capital*) that inform their capacities for writing center work in the first place; (2) to activism and its implications for participants' sites, bodies, tutors, students, and the discipline; and (3) to site-based, interpersonal, and disciplinary tensions (which often take the form of bullying and mobbing) that surface in connection with participants' queer bodies. While the study draws from the wisdom of queer laborers, this is, first and foremost, a book about writing center administration; it is for writing center practitioners of all orientations, queer and nonqueer alike. Writing center directors identify as LGBTQA more frequently than national averages (Valles, Babcock, and Jackson 2017), and while many of the book's arguments surround issues of queer communities, I have written with the intention of speaking at once to queer and nonqueer audiences about writing center work. Ultimately, this book offers practitioners a heuristic for understanding and complicating work, for seeing a nuanced queer vision for it, and for seeing themselves in this book regardless of their sexuality.

CULTURAL CONTEXT

Research about queer identity and writing center administration is timely in that the Western political landscape is complexly nuanced for queer people—unprecedentedly progressive yet codedly and explicitly oppressive and violent. On one hand, a June 2013 Supreme Court of the United States (SCOTUS) decision on *United States v. Windsor* overturned the Defense of Marriage Act (DOMA) of 1996, while a June 2015 SCOTUS ruling on *Obergefell v. Hodges* extended marriage equality nationally. Such instances are not insignificant, certainly for those who remember the passing of DOMA or who experienced the legal limbo of same-sex partnerships between 2013 and 2015. On the other hand, queer people who do not enjoy privileged access feel the impact of local and national injustices, such as queer and transgender homelessness in historically queer neighborhoods; queer and transgender suicide in urban and rural centers; erasure of queer and transgender people of color from legislative activism at local and national levels; and the national attention resulting from many mandates, such Houston's Equal Rights Ordinance, that seek to protect queer people from discriminatory practices but that are often met with phobia, contestation, and controversy. The weight of violence toward queer people is especially heavy as well, as the *Pulse* shooting and regular queer and transgender murders point to.

In November 2016, the presidential election complicated such a landscape for queer people. Despite the former executive administration's lip service to business as usual for queers and marriage equality, the then-president, on more than one occasion, Tweeted transphobic statements, some directed at active military and veteran transgender people (Trump 2017). And yet, on May 31, 2019, one day before the start of World Pride month, Trump tweeted,

> As we celebrate LGBT Pride Month and recognize the outstanding contributions LGBT people have made to our great Nation, let us also stand in solidarity with the many LGBT people who live in dozens of countries

worldwide that punish, imprison, or even execute individuals . . . on the basis of their sexual orientation. (2019)

Trump's prideful back pat isn't entirely unwarranted: at face value, the United States is not a country that explicitly imprisons or executes queer people. Yet, this administration's executive orders and closest appointees did much harm to queer people, which extended into Trump's 2020 homophobic and transphobic sentiments and actions that mirrored those of his early presidency: people of his ilk propel forward a narrow definition of religious freedom at the expense of queer people and care little for addressing, or even acknowledging, everyday oppressions that impact queer and transgender people, such as work-based discrimination. When I started writing this book, a queer person could be fired from a job for being LGBTQA in forty-eight of fifty states. Allowing a glimmer of queer hope, however, the SCOTUS recently heard *Bostock v. Clayton County, Georgia,* and *Altitude Express, Inc. v. Zarda and R. G. & G. R. Harris Funeral Homes v. EEOC* to make decisions about federal work protections for LGBTQA people. Despite a conservatively packed SCOTUS with recent Trump justice appointees, the court ruled six to three that the sex-based workplace discrimination applies to gay, lesbian, and transgender workers, thus making on-the-job discrimination against gay, lesbian, and transgender people unconstitutional (Totenberg 2020).

DEFINING LABOR BEYOND AND WITHIN WRITING CENTERS

Work and *labor*—two words used interchangeably throughout this book—are about our professions, our day and night[4] jobs, and our production. In his work on burnout in rhetoric and composition, James Daniel (2020) identifies distinctions between work and labor, arguing that "labor is associated with production" while "work names the conditions and locations of labor." These distinctions are important yet difficult to parse out alongside the complexities of participant stories about their writing center leadership, which informs my rhetorical decision to use the words somewhat interchangeably throughout this book. In this book, *work* and *labor* are what these queer writing center administrators do *for a living,* as we might say in Western culture, in order to signal the oft-recognized relationship between performing labor and being a worker within an industry for the purposes of capital exchange and personal and professional livelihood. Arguably, industrialist and capitalist economies gave rise to our present definitions of work and identity, informing modern conceptions of, for example, *emotional labor* and *gig economy* that span industries. One would only need to scan the *Chronicle of Higher Education* to see the words *work* or *labor* operationalized and contextualized alongside any number of professional issues, from adjunct and contingent labor to identity, justice, equity, and access in universities.

Journalism and more popularized media do not shy away from such embodied conversations: Barbara Ehrenreich's (2001, 2005) research showcases early intersections of work, class, access, and privilege of Western, modern labor forces, while David Shipler's (2004) *The Working Poor: Invisible in America* won a Pulitzer Prize, signaling scholarly and journalistic focuses on work, access, and the people who are laboring. As Western culture advances into late capitalism—or the chaos comprising global work lives that surfaces from the violence of capitalism, taken up and popularized from Ernest Mandel's 1975 *Late Capitalism*—we, as global citizens, see the realities of labor landscapes, sometimes exciting, sometimes bleak, a vacillating theme that arises in this book.

Work and labor surface in Arlie Hochschild's (1979) critical sociological research. Hochshild showcases the gendered work of flight attendants, work not included in their official job descriptions but that is a no less laborious form of capital exchange, whether it is smiling or keeping customers happy while in flight. From that study, she argues that work and workers labor far beyond documented job duties, as this book argues. Alongside Hochschild, this book's labor definitions, by default, align with social sciences research grounded in *visible* and *invisible labor* (Daniels 1987; Crain, Poster, and Cherry 2016). Drawing from these theorists, I define *visible labor* as nameable, countable, measurable, and translatable to a job description for which a laborer is compensated and evaluated, whereas *invisible labor* accounts for work not often associated with, understood, or recognized as explicitly generating capital for an institution but that capitalizes on the emotional and embodied work of its laborers. This labor, however invisible, however emotional, and however unaccounted for does indeed propel forward institutions, often at workers' emotional and embodied expense. Such labor definitions inform the double-edged sword of this book's queer workers' often invisible and sometimes visible work. On one hand, this book's chapters teach us these directors are primed for and are the best advocates for carrying out particular kinds of writing center labor. For example, many participants note a likelihood that tutors and students alike will look to them for mental- and sexual-health support and advice. These directors' writing centers often act as queer de facto sites for medical- and sexual-health support when other university resources fail to materialize. Such labors are often gratifying but also occasionally trying for participants, as articulated in later chapters. Despite its tensions, no participant would entirely forego such invisible labors, minus the bullying, but it is worth mentioning that this work falls with intensity on these queer practitioners. Difficulty arises in the fact that such work is also difficult to name, categorize, and document for professional advancement and disciplinary participation and forward movement.

Grutsch McKinney's (2013) *Peripheral Visions for Writing Centers* opening recounts the familiar forms of work writing center directorships entail, whether writing, reading, researching, mentoring, consulting, advocating, scheduling, tutoring, meeting, talking, or worrying (1–2). Directors lead their sites and develop, implement, and assess their missions. They teach tutoring courses. They manage budgets and payroll. They tutor and help tutors tutor. They manage conflict. They listen, they talk, and they mentor. This book's participants do this work, yet their labor also departs distinctly from what we, in the writing center world, talk about when we talk about writing center work: participant work extends beyond the field's researched parameters when, for example, a queer writing center director is the first to hear about a queer tutor's suicidal ideation, or when a tutor comes out as gay, transgender, or polyamorous and seeks a queer director's immediate support. Or when the queer writing center director is the "go-to" person for all things queer on campus, like students' experiences with sexual assault or tutors' fears about the Trump administration's impact on queer and transgender communities. Or when participant Jeremy tells me our writing centers are not merely sites where queer activism may happen but are spaces uniquely and queerly conducive to such endeavors, especially through tutor-training courses and empirical research. Or when it is up to participant Madeline to make the case to a workshop participant that conversations about gender-neutral pronouns matter to writing center work.

In this sense, participants certainly do work that translates to recent writing center administrative-labor research, especially emotional and everyday and disciplinary labor (Caswell, Grutsch McKinney, and Jackson 2016, 23–27) or everyday and intellectual labor (Geller and Denny 2013). These researchers define labor as work that represents practitioners' job descriptions, their scholarly participation and production, and their mediation and resolution within interpersonal professional contexts (Caswell, Grutsch McKinney, and Jackson 2016, 27; Geller and Denny 2013). Yet, I depart somewhat from Caswell, Grutsch McKinney, and Jackson's (2016) definitions for their participants' "emotional labor," or "work that involves care, mentoring, or nurturing of others; work of building and sustaining relationships; work to resolve conflicts;

managing our display of emotion" (27). I find significant value in Caswell, Grutsch McKinney, and Jackson's study and in how they name participant work. But I hesitate to call my book's participants' work "emotional labor." This is not to say the participant labor isn't without emotional impact, nor that it departs completely from Caswell, Grutsch McKinney, and Jackson's definitions.

Rather than completely adopt this term—*emotional labor*—I prefer to extend forward these recently defined labor taxonomies, for emotional labor is not easily delineated from other forms of labor (everyday or disciplinary), nor does the term account for the labor of merely living in a queer body as a writing center administrator, given the national landscapes described earlier in this book's introduction. As this book delves into in later chapters, *emotional labor* as a descriptor does not neatly help some queer participants make sense of on-the-job violence inflicted upon them. For example, as theorized in chapter 4, some participants' most laborious work stems from being bullied. The bullying, its consequences, and its participant responses, whether through pushback or silence, are not merely consequential offshoots of the work but work itself that interfaces and complicates participants' official job duties. Facing and working alongside colleagues who, for example, have called you a "fag" is its own kind of labor. To do one's work alongside such landscapes, among many other examples outlined in later chapters framed in *capital, activism,* and *tension,* is also such a labor—an invisible labor—that we in the writing center field have not explicitly addressed in scholarship, except on occasion at our national venues, which by and large, and by definition, are exclusive sites.

WRITING CENTER ADMINISTRATIVE WORK AND
QUEER IDENTITY: A RESEARCH GLIMPSE

Labor discussions intersect with higher education and, by extension, writing center administration. In this regard, any writing center administrator experiences a host of day-in-the-life interactions that shed light on the current political sphere. The quotidian instances—good, bad, ugly—of our writing centers are never too distant from the zeitgeist of the national landscape (Denny 2010, 2011, 2014; Denny et al. 2019; Hallman Martini and Webster 2017b). In essence, what happens in the world at large also happens to us as professionals. This dynamic is especially true for queer writing center administrators who may navigate a landscape, both on the job and in the world, wherein progression, regression, and oppression exist simultaneously. On the job, queer professionals may exercise rights in naming same-sex spouses in work-related documents and protocol, like medical insurance, next-of-kin status, and tax dependency but still may feel the emotional weight of lived experiences in leading writing centers and bridging and living professional and personal lives. Take, for instance, the queer director who overhears homophobic or transphobic hate speech in the center; the gay job candidate who meets raised eyebrows after mentioning a same-sex spouse during a research talk; the trans administrator who fears material repercussions of merely existing on campus and using public facilities, no matter how Leftist the institution may seem; the queer administrator of color who experiences coded racism in departmental meetings while also facing a landscape where gender identity and sexual orientation don't exist in their university's diversity policies or nondiscrimination language. As this book argues in later chapters, such landscapes not only impact queer work but also create circumstances that are, in fact, work.

Work and Labor Research and/in Writing Centers

As of late, labor surfaces as a critical research area in writing center studies. The field's recent award-winning text and a key inspiration for this book, *The Working Lives of New Writing Center Directors*, mentioned earlier, examines case studies and extensive interviews with nine new professionals directing writing centers (Caswell, Grutsch McKinney, and Jackson 2016). In it, the authors offer specific labor definitions that speak to the state of twenty-first-century writing center work. The work—"everyday," "disciplinary," and "emotional" labor—refers to that of job descriptions, independent and collaborative scholarship and research, and the "care, mentoring, or nurturing of others" (27). This rich study stems from a tradition, often grounded in survey-based and theoretical pieces, that traces who writing center directors are and what they do (Balester and McDonald 2001; Crisp 2000; Elliott 1990; Fels et al. 2016; Healy 1995; Ianetta et al. 2006; Isaacs and Knight 2014; Lerner 2006; Mattison 2011; Valles, Babcock, and Jackson 2017), alongside key national surveys that trace administrator backgrounds nationally, among other data (National Census of Writing n.d.; Writing Centers Research Project n.d.).

The Working Lives of New Writing Center Directors (2016) aligns with another recent award-winning, labor-focused text no less critical to this book, "Of Ladybugs, Low Status, and Loving the Job: Writing Center Professionals Navigating Their Careers," with the latter study focused on thirteen interviews about work with writing center directors who attended or were affiliated with the 2005 IWCA SI. In it, Anne Ellen Geller and Harry Denny (2013), similar to Caswell, Grutsch McKinney, and Jackson (2016), trace writing center director work, focusing on how forms of labor—"intellectual" and "everyday" (102–4)—impact the establishment and sustainability of writing center directors' research production, which, both studies claim, is made difficult because of laborious administrative conditions that take precedence over academic production—a reality with individual and collective disciplinary implications. Both studies allude to chasms in their data, noting that work could very well be complicated by participant subjectivity. In fact, *The Working Lives of New Writing Center Directors* (Caswell, Grutsch McKinney, and Jackson 2016) concludes with the "unsaid" of participant work, especially that "[the researchers] expected would enter [their] conversations," like "gender, race, sexuality, religion, (dis)abilities, marital or family status, or social class" (180) but which participants did not share or note as relevant. For the researchers, such identity-based omissions on the part of new writing center directors point to the occasion: the researchers themselves didn't ask, but participants may have withheld this information intentionally, assuming it irrelevant to work, perceiving it outside the research scope, or other such factors (180). These participant omissions are unsurprising, as such conversations are not often on the radar of disciplinary research despite writing center directors identifying as LGBTQA more frequently than national averages (Valles, Babcock, and Jackson 2017), as stated earlier.

LGBTQA Issues and/in Writing Centers

Framed explicitly in queer and sexuality studies among other intersectional tenets, a fall 2017 *Peer Review* special issue, "Writing Centers as Brave/r Spaces" (Hallman Martini and Webster 2017b), showcases empirical, theoretical, and narrative works, arguing that writing centers exist, conflict, and thrive within the current political landscape. The collection itself holds the most writing center-focused collection of queer pieces in one place, with four articles that deal explicitly with queer bodies, orientations, and studies for writing center work (Dixon 2017; Faison and Trevino 2017; Hermann 2017; McNamee and Miley 2017). Yet, queer subjectivity and writing center work are still underexamined and undertheorized in writing center research.

In fact, a key critical glimpse into the intersection of queer and writing center studies, Andrew Rihn and Jay Sloan's (2013) "Rainbows in the Past Were Gay: LGBTQIA in the WC," argues that queer research "relating to sexual identity" in writing centers is quite sparse, especially given emphasis on writing center investigation into "structural inequalities" framed in other identity markers such as "sex, race, class, and dis/ability" (1). I depart slightly with Rihn and Sloan's claim in that I don't necessarily agree that these latter subjectivities are given adequate attention in writing center scholarship. Yet, I agree with their expression of both "pride and disappointment" (1): pride in what queer or LGBTQA writing center research does exist alongside disappointment because of a lack of investigation into queer issues and bodies in writing center research as a whole. Even their piece that traces silence, heteronormativity, and erasure across writing center research identifies rich queer writing center content and also reveals a scarcity of explicit queer research specific to writing centers. Which is not to say queer issues are not part of the conversation alongside and since Rihn and Sloan's (2013) discussions, in that Michele Eodice (2010), Jonathan Doucette (2011), Rexford Rose (2016), and Jonathan J. Rylander (2017) critically examine queer theories and writing center praxis, specifically in regard to writing center spaces and tutoring practices. Further, Jay Sloan himself authored the writing center field's earliest LGBTQA scholarship about writing tutoring (1997, 2003, 2004).

Front and center in Rihn and Sloan's (2013) examination is Harry Denny's (2005, 2011, 2013) work. Signaling the affordances of operationalizing queer theory in writing center spaces, Denny (2005) suggests such a framework is critical to writing center work. But it is, perhaps, Denny's (2011) book-length theoretical study, *Facing the Center: Toward an Identity Politics of One-to-One Mentoring*, that acts as the writing center field's primary text about a spectrum of intersectionalities related to writing center work. In it, he positions centers—one-on-one peer tutoring in particular—as sites always already about identity and intersectionality. Denny frames the text in his "epiphany—that identity politics are real and uncharted in writing centers" (4), rightly and beautifully articulating that "a day doesn't go by that somebody [in a writing center] doesn't contend with the dilemma of assimilating, going with the flow, or challenging the well-worn path" (16). These three frameworks guide his discussions through writing centers and issues of gender, sexuality, race, class, ability, and nationality. While Denny (2011) delves into various subjectivities, his gender and sex chapter makes way for such conversations in the first place, arguably for the first time in writing center studies, alongside rhetoric and composition research framed in sexual literacies and writing practices (Alexander 2008). Yet, *Facing the Center* (2011) is not necessarily empirically framed in queer bodies that inhabit writing center spaces but is more situated in queer, queered, and queering orientations to the assimilationist and subversive potential of writing center work within institutions of higher education.

A recent sister text to *Facing the Center, Out in the Center: Public Controversies and Private Struggles* (Denny et al. 2019), an edited collection, marks intersectional, autoethnographic voices coalesced to make concrete many of the theoretical underpinnings of *Facing the Center*. Whereas *Facing the Center* (2011) theorizes from one scholarly vantage point, *Out in the Center* (2019) showcases writing center voices of myriad identity intersections around issues of public discourse and writing center work. These two texts' foundations in postmodern writing center work are certainly grounded in Nancy Grimm's (1999) *Good Intentions: Writing Center Work for Postmodern Times*, which inspired writing center texts similar in sentiment, such as *Noise from the Center* (Boquet 2002), *The Everyday Writing Center* (Geller, Eodice, Condon, Carroll, and Boquet 2007), *Writing Centers and the New Racism* (Greenfield and Rowan 2011), *The Writing Center as Cultural and Interdisciplinary Contact Zone* (Monty 2016), and *Radical Writing Center Practice* (Greenfield 2019). Aligned with such conversations, *Queerly Centered* also seeks to contribute to the disciplinary lineage that understands and positions writing center work and sites beyond tutoring.

This book delves into racial dynamics, as two participants are of color and many are intersectionally embodied in their queerness (e.g., queer *and* black; queer *and* female; queer *and* transgender; queer *and* gender nonconforming). In this sense, this book is in conversation with such recent works as Riddick and Hooker's (2019) *Praxis: A Writing Center Journal's* special issue "Race in the Writing Center," Romeo Garcia's (2017) "Unmaking Gringo Centers," and Neisha-Anne Green's (2018) influential *Writing Center Journal* article calling for accompliceship over alliance. In fact, Green's call to action around "word and deed" (29) inspires this book's directions for communication with both queer and nonqueer audiences in that accompliceship within raced, homophobic, and transphobic landscapes is of utmost importance for this book. Said another way, Green, when calling white colleagues to action on behalf of writing center practitioners of color, argues that white people being supposed allies to people of color isn't enough. She sees disparity between what people say and what they do. In this sense, she calls for an accompliceship of *doing* the work of supporting and advocating for colleagues of color in national and disciplinary landscapes that are often on a sliding scale between untoward to violent. In the spirit of this conversation, Garcia (2017) points out that the writing center field must complicate its raced understandings beyond Black-White dynamics, which ultimately erases writing center stakeholders with diversely and intersectionally raced bodies. Such conversations mirror those present in the work of

Vershawn Anthony Young's (2011), Anne Geller, Frankie Condon, and Meg Carroll's (2011), and several scholars' race-focused scholarship in Laura Greenfield and Karen Rowan's collection, *Writing Centers and the New Racism: A Call for Sustainable Dialogue and Change* (2011), as well as the antiracism work of Wonderful Faison, Talisha Haltiwanger Morrison, Katie Levin, Elijah Simmons, Jasmine Kar Tang, and Keli Tucker (2019) that stems from IWCA antiracism missions.

Rhetoric and composition subfields have empirical and theoretical roots in labor and queer, raced, or intersectional personhood as well. In the technical communication field, Matthew B. Cox (2019) examines how queer corporate workers navigate and name the public and private in their professional lives. Staci Perryman-Clark and Collin Lamott Craig's (2019a) *Black Perspectives in Writing Program Administration: From Margins to the Center* offers a collection of Black voices that call for intersectional intra- and intercoalition building for writing studies administrators (i.e., workers) within writing program administration and rhetoric and composition. Genevieve Garcia de Mueller and Iris Ruiz (2016) and Sandra Tarabochia (2016, 2017) engage with person-based research about university faculty to bring raced and gendered perspectives to writing program administration and writing across the curriculum. And the writing program administration world has, indeed, delved into queer identity, queer work, and queer issues (Alexander 2009; Alexander and Banks 2009; Banks 2012; Denny 2013; Kopelson 2013; Pauliny 2011; Rhodes 2010) through studies that examine queer administrative positionality, queering of the WPA discipline and statements, and queer subversions through administration while not necessarily offering empirically driven studies, as this book does.

LABOR, CONTINGENCY, AND IDENTITY WITHIN AND BEYOND WRITING CENTERS

Contingency in writing centers and higher education, while not this book's focal point, does intersect with its research framework. Dawn Fels, Clint Gardener, Maggie Herb, and Liliana Naydan (2016), for example, conduct qualitative, person-based research on contingent (i.e., non-tenure-track) writing center directors' labor, tracing the broader impact of such labor on the writing center field, including its workers and its stakeholders. Discussions of contingency are not too far from issues of retention and sustainability—two secondary themes of this book—especially as we, in both the writing center and rhetoric and composition fields, consider and act on behalf of the long-term sustainability of our writing sites, our research, and our place within higher education. As such, higher education practitioners regularly question higher education's long-term sustainability, anticipating its eventual collapse per our lack of critical, proactive, and progressive orientation to work and workers. It is a tumultuous landscape where workers and work are subject to and punished by neoliberal institutions of late capitalism. Rhetoric and composition studies of the past decade, especially those published during or after the 2008 American stock-market crash, speak to conversations of contingency (Bousquet 2008; Carter 2008; Kahn, Lalicker, and Lynch-Biniek 2017; Strickland 2011). This project does deal explicitly with a sister conversation about contingency (i.e., worker retention) related to the invisible, intensive labor of queer writing center directors and its long-term impact on workers, work, and universities. Which is to say this book, while focused on writing centers, may help practitioners navigate the rhetoric and composition world's contingency research and is marginally in conversation with work such as Fels et al.'s (2016) research.

METHODS

With a 2016 International Writing Centers Association (IWCA) Research Grant, I conducted twenty interviews, following Institutional Review Board approval from my previous institution. Semistructured interviews based on eight open-ended questions[5] ranged from approximately thirty minutes to an hour and a half, with broad questions focused on participant perspectives about queer identity and writing center administration. I first invited queer writing center practitioners who were "out" either through their research or site missions and who held full-time administrative or faculty roles at collegiate writing centers, but I recruited a majority through snowball sampling and the 2016 and 2017 IWCA conferences. I recorded interviews with my personal phone and my MacBook's Garage Band application. Using the recordings, I took notes on each interview, logging notable selections and writing short vignettes about each participant. I later had the interviews professionally transcribed, coding those transcriptions using NVivo10 for MAC. I ran data queries on NVivo to identify emerging data patterns, first relying on participants' oft-used and notable key words or phrases. Using words and phrases, I coded the transcripts for participants' descriptions and discussions of and reactions to work they did as their site's lead administrator.

This book showcases twenty queer voices across the nation across many institutions and subject positions. Among these voices were many complementary threads that arose from coding and analysis. I do not intend, however, to argue that these data are so generalizable as to capture the work experiences of any and all queer writing center directors. Yet I do think this book's emergent theories can still teach practitioners about writing center administrative labor. In this sense, this project is empirical, qualitative, and, perhaps, somewhat replicable, aggregable, and data driven (RAD). In some ways, RAD is a fabulous lens for conducting writing center research. In other ways, I believe it poses problems with regard to identity ethics for both researchers and participants. From a RAD lens, my methods are replicable, and I do hope they could offer a lens for other queer, transgender, and raced projects. However, I caution against just any researcher replicating my methods and instruments given that my queer body played a critical role in the development and framework for the project, including and especially linked to recruitment and establishing trust with my participants. In this sense, I rely on Alexandria Lockett's (2019) guidance from her qualitative work with Black writing center stakeholders. In her chapter in *Out in the Center: Public Controversies and Private Struggles*, "A Touching Place: Womanist Approaches to the Center," she cautions against an overreliance on RAD methodologies, arguing that RAD "tends to strip the human experience of its nuance and may risk diminishing the various ways we might interpret experience as data" (33). Lockett draws from Neil Simpkins and Virginia Schwarz (2015), who do believe RAD methods can be effectively, productively, and queerly queered, but begin their now-landmark writing center blog post, "Queering RAD in Writing Center Studies," with concerns about how queer and transgender bodies, ontologies, and ideologies may be uncomplimentary to RAD methods, which often don't account for the fluid nature of person-based research. This study's methods rest on these researchers' claims in that I don't believe RAD methods are the best lens for a book about queer working bodies and stories. Further, as Lockett (2019) suggests, I don't believe generalizability is possible, nor the point, when so few queer empirical writing center studies exist in the first place (a claim she makes about the dearth of writing center scholarship focused on Black writing center stakeholders). Despite this RAD critique, I do, however, feel an empirical, qualitative glimpse into these voices offers these queer perspectives a disciplinary credibility of sorts. It is worth a mention here that much of what exists about the conversations of this book exists primarily in field lore (i.e., in listserv conversations, in bar conversations at conferences, and in LGBTQA special-interest groups at conferences). While lore isn't a bad thing necessarily, an empirical glimpse through coded data about queer writing center work and workers may actually better support and showcase the labor and laborers of this book, moving such conversations out of listserv conversations, conference bars, and special-interest groups and into published writing center scholarship—and, more importantly, into our centers and the broader field.

This book's participants identify as gay, lesbian, transgender, and queer across intersections of race, class, gender, and background. I interviewed only writing center directors, assistant directors, coordinators, and professionals who hold nongraduate student leadership status in writing centers (i.e., I did not interview graduate students or graduate assistants who work in writing centers). Participants hail from varied institution types, whether research extensive, regional comprehensive, community college, small or large private, or secondary education and hold diverse institutional roles, whether tenure stream, tenured, or full-time administrative.

This book, as evidenced in table 0.1 below, showcases the voices of ten participants who are male identifying and gay; nine who are female identifying and lesbian or queer; and one who is transgender/female-to-male and opposite-sex oriented. Despite a lack of gender and racial diversity in the writing center world, I was able to recruit participants across male- and female-identifying participants. Sarah Banschbach Valles, Rebecca Day Babcock, and Karen Keaton Jackson (2017) reveal, from 313 survey responses about national writing center demographics, that 91.3 percent of participants were white, 71.5 percent female, and 28.5 percent male—percentages that reflect the field's few studies. I point to Valles, Babcock and Keaton's project to note a lack of diversity, showing that, despite the writing center world being homogenous across race and gender (i.e., made up of mostly white, straight, female practitioners), this book does offer some diversity of voice.

With this said, even with snowball sampling and my own active recruitment at conferences special interest groups, I was not able to diversify my pool enough to get more than one transgender voice. Yet, while just one participant identifies as transgender, other participants do identify themselves or their practices as gender nonconforming—a gender expression that refuses traditional conceptions and performances of norms associated with being male and being female in Western culture. And, despite a typical "sea of white" participant Matt describes in the lobby of his first IWCA conference and that pervades the writing center field, I did recruit two gay men of color. I asked both for support in snowball sampling. Both were open to doing so, but struggled to name other queer people of color who direct writing centers. As is, this study includes just these two voices of color, though neither are women of color (I speak more about this limitation in this book's conclusion). Similarly, I attempted to consciously avoid bisexual and asexual erasure—common forms of erasure in the LGBTQA community—but was not able to recruit participants who identified explicitly as bisexual or asexual, though many participants spoke about stories, experiences, or contexts that alluded to bisexuality and asexuality.

All participants noted no problem with their names being used in this project, as most align with the mantra that the personal is the political (and further, the professional and the administrative). However, participants hold varied relationships to current and past institutions and myriad position types, with some positions more secure than others. For these reasons, I yielded to giving pseudonyms in that participants may not always hold the same stances about anonymity given prospective professional and personal changes that may arise later.

Table 0.1 doesn't do justice to participant voices. For that reason, their voices frame the next chapters, which name, analyze, and situate their queer work.

ANALYSIS

I relied on rhetoric and composition's feminist rhetorical research practices and methodologies about uncovering and showcasing voices yet unheard in published scholarship (Royster and Kirsch 2012). I did my best to listen to and for these queer voices. I was able to do so, in part, because of my queer body attuned to exclusions in broader Western cultures, which is to say that what's erased in culture writ large may also mirror exclusions in the profession, despite the writing center world's mostly queer-friendly orientations to research and praxis. The voices and lenses of this project are not only unheard but are often silenced with the word *lore*, a well-intentioned word that makes its way into writing center research methods as of late. I myself do not take issue with the idea of disciplinary "lore" in the ways accounts of recent writing center research about methods have[6] (Driscoll and Perdue 2012). Because of my cultural rhetorics training at Michigan State University, I find stories help researchers both frame and extrapolate theory. I would go so far as to say, as cultural rhetorics scholars long have said (Bratta and Powell 2016; Brooks-Gillies 2018; Powell et al. 2014), that stories are, in fact, theory.

When working with and writing about transgender voices, I used G Patterson's (2019) theoretical, ethical frameworks for analysis and

Table 0.1. Participant Demographics

Name	Identification	Gender	Race	Position	Institution	Region
Adam	Gay	Male identifying	White	Part-time administrator & adjunct faculty	Community college	Northeast
Amanda	Queer	Female identifying	White	Staff administrator & adjunct faculty	Community college	Midwest
Dana	Queer	Gender nonconforming	White	Staff administrator	Research	Northeast
Brian	Gay	Male identifying	Black	Tenured faculty administrator	Regional comprehensive	North/Midwest
Casey	Pansexual	Female identifying	White	Pretenure faculty administrator	Private	Southeast
Cara	Lesbian	Female identifying	White	Non-tenure-track faculty administrator and instructional faculty	Research	North/Midwest
David	Gay	Male identifying	White	Tenured faculty administrator	Community college	North/Midwest
Jack	Transgender	Male identifying	White	Staff administrator & adjunct faculty	Private	Midwest
James	Gay	Male identifying	Black	Staff administrator	Community college	North
Jennifer	Lesbian	Female identifying	White	Staff administrator	Regional comprehensive	Northeast
Jeremy	Gay	Male identifying	White	Pretenure faculty administrator	Regional comprehensive	North
John	Gay	Male identifying	White	Tenured faculty administrator	Research	Southeast
Katherine	Lesbian	Female identifying	White	Staff administrator and instructional faculty	Research	North/Midwest
Leah	Lesbian	Female identifying	White	Staff administrator and adjunct faculty	Research	North
Madeline	Lesbian	Female identifying	White	Tenured faculty administrator	Research	South
Matt	Gay	Male identifying	White	Part-time faculty administrator	Secondary education	North

continued on next page

Table 0.1—*continued*

Name	Identification	Gender	Race	Position	Institution	Region
Mike	Gay	Male identifying	White	Tenured faculty administrator	Research	North/ Midwest
Ryan	Gay	Male identifying	White	Staff administrator & non-TT faculty	Research	Northeast
Stephanie	Lesbian	Gender nonconforming	White	Staff administrator & adjunct faculty	Regional comprehensive	South
Tim	Gay	Male identifying	White	Tenured faculty administrator	Regional comprehensive	North/ Midwest

composition. Patterson (2019), a transgender rhetoric and composition researcher, calls cisgender scholars to abandon "performative allyship," to direct their privileged bodies instead to acting as "co-conspirators," understanding that allyship is mere lip service given the oppressive and violent global landscapes for transgender people. In other words, only collective conspiring against such landscapes is beneficial to and saves transgender people from material harm. From this methodological approach, Patterson offers several ethical parameters that ought to be engaged when and before cisgender people write about transgender people. Their call includes owning one's cisgender privilege, enacting transgender reciprocity, exhibiting transcultural competency, and "amplifying" trans voices, first and foremost (Patterson 2019). In aligning my writing-based and analytic frameworks with Patterson's rightful and apt call, I first name my cisgender privilege here, as I am a gay, white, cisgender male whose lived experiences offer me privilege as well as a distinct departure from what transgender people live and face in their daily lives, especially their professional lives—this book's guiding landscape. I have done my best to "amplify" the critical voice of Jack, the book's transgender participant, in order to propel forward writing center research, which has not yet showcased trans voices with rigor. I hope this project and others that follow it might change that scholarly landscape, which is how I think about reciprocity with transgender scholars in writing centers, especially Jack. In interviewing and writing about him, I have also used his preferred pronouns (i.e., he, him, and his), in order to write transcompetently on his behalf, as Patterson (2019) suggests.

Similarly, in working alongside, drawing from, and writing about queer Black voices, I write with attention to Eric Darnell Prichard's (2019) guest blog post on Carmen Kynard's "Education, Liberation, and Black Radical Traditions from the Twenty-First Century" blog. In it, Pritchard calls attention to Black queer femme and female erasure in rhetoric and composition, referring first to the 2019 distribution of a *Literacy in Composition Studies* call for papers (CFP) that was pulled, revised, and redistributed because of its Black erasure and transexclusionarity in framework and citations. Prichard (2019) notes that despite revisions to the CFP, it still glaringly excludes several rhetoric and composition women of color and queer people of color. Mindful of Pritchard's (2019) concerns and frustrations, I write this book with attention to ethically showcasing and writing about the Black queers in this study and also commit to citing and recognizing Black queer scholarship. A tension, however, examined throughout this book is that writing center scholarship has not adequately delved into race in writing centers; in fact, race is often superficially examined in writing center studies, as Romeo Garcia (2017) so richly argues in his investigation into Mexican American writing center frameworks that complicate the field's attention to Black-White dichotomies. Thus, in adding to commitment, I have sought to be an accomplice (Green 2018; Patterson 2019) to Black (and transgender) voices through this book in addressing what's just not there in writing center research, as many participants relay.

ABOUT THIS BOOK

The previous section's chart includes participants' self-identifications, which span the LGBTQA identity spectrum. Throughout this book, however, I use *queer* as an interchangeable stand-in for LGBTQA. I am aware personally and professionally that the word *queer* holds distinct histories and meanings that do not always align with Western culture's LGBTQA acronym. With this said, *queer* on the page is more readable than *LGBTQA*. Further, I use the words *director, administrator, practitioner,* and *professional* rather interchangeably in this book to describe people who officially lead writing centers. Because the book is about how leaders lead, I worried about using just one signifier, simply because of readability and repetition. For example, I didn't want the word *director* to be in every third sentence, hence my reliance on other similar terms. I realize the field has taken up this administrative distinction (Caswell, Grutsch McKinney, and Jackson 2016; Geller and Denny 2013) and encourages scholars to be intentional when referring to our writing center work, as

I have done my best to be. Further, *work* and *labor* are used somewhat interchangeably through this book, despite historical and etymological nuances of each term discussed earlier in this chapter.

BOOK ARC AND CHAPTER SUMMARIES

This book's chapters offer a narrative arc that rests and draws upon participant voices. Each chapter begins with historical vignettes that introduce and connect to chapter themes and that showcase participants beyond this introduction's participant chart. Its three analytic chapters begin with how participants first oriented to their writing center work (what chapter 2 calls "capital," "origins," and "readiness") in order to situate participant histories. Using these histories for further labor discussions (chapter 2, in fact, argues that participant capital, origins, and readiness are their own form of labor), chapter 3 examines and analyzes how participants are drawn and led, if not pressured, to respond to local, national, and disciplinary calls for writing center activism; it is their capital and histories that sometimes led them to this work in the first place. The chapter explicitly examines the work of these practitioners and its personal, political, and disciplinary impact on participants, their sites, and the writing center field. Discussions of activism lead to chapter 4, which focuses on how participants experience tensions, especially bullying, in their positions.

Chapter 2: Queer Writing Center Labor and/as Capital

Chapter 2 examines the origins and histories of how queer participants come to know, understand, and labor in their writing center administrative positions. Participants discuss relationships among their former or current lives as activists, teachers, organizers, and myriad careers grounded in their queer identities. One participant recalls being prepared for writing center work long before he entered the field by his work with people as an early AIDS-era community organizer—a role, he claims, mirrors the work of a writing center practitioner (i.e., working with people "where they are" and supporting their long-term sexual education as a big-picture learning process). Other participants note leadership and experiences in organizations and sites—such as the Girl Scouts of America and growing up gay in the South—that queerly inform their pedagogical approaches and give way to later administrative understandings, what the chapter calls *capital*. Participants name and exhibit a rhetorical readiness for writing center administrative work. The readiness itself calls forth Pierre Bourdieu's (1986) and R. Mark

Hall's (2010) definitions and applications of cultural and social capital, through which I examine how queer practitioners draw from queer lives to make sense of, navigate, survive, and thrive within writing centers as people of difference, often respected yet sometimes feared in their institutions of higher education.

Chapter 3: Queer Writing Center Labor and/as Activism

Extending the writing center field's engagements with writing centers as sites of activism and bravery, chapter 3 analyzes how participants articulate, enact, respond to, and feel about how their professional identities and sites interface with forms of activism, whether locally, glocally, or globally. Writing centers as sites of activism and civic engagement pervade current disciplinary conversations—from peer-reviewed research (Denny 2011; Green 2018; Hallman Martini and Webster 2017b; Ozias and Godbee 2011) to quotidian listserv conversations. Such conversations imply that writing centers ought, in the first place, to uphold and sustain justice-focused orientations and that the writing center field's few diverse leaders ought to lead such activism on- and off-site from their writing centers. The chapter analyzes the perspectives of labor and activism as they play out in the lives of queer administrators of varied ranks, institutions, backgrounds, and orientations given that all twenty participants allude to, comment on, or expound upon it. Participants report myriad experiences ranging from supporting tutors and writers with politically driven documents, arguments, and processes to helping writing center and university communities cope with major events, like Orlando's 2016 *Pulse* nightclub shooting of queer people, the account of which opened this book. Such instances offer participants professional moments of resolve that, they report, contribute to a greater good. Queer writing center administrators may revel in such activist orientations to writing center administration, but it is no less a form of distinct, nuanced, and often invisible labor than is emotional labor, which has been outlined by nonqueer colleagues in past and recent writing center administrative literature. Without collective sharing of such labor across institutions and disciplines, the writing center field's articulated values may be unsustainable and unattainable. Further, the work of writing center activism and advocacy often falls on some of the field's most vulnerable. From an activist standpoint, I argue that a social justice orientation to writing center work is not the rhetorical and administrative responsibility of only administrators of difference and diversity. Given that many participants, especially queer participants of color and trans participants, discuss the glaring absence of queer, trans, and POC voices and projects in writing center studies, I further suggest that accomplice-ship (Green 2018) is a critical method for thinking about and moving writing center studies and research forward. The "sea of white and straight" (i.e., how one participant describes the annual writing center flagship conference) may not offer a sustainable landscape and may directly contradict values the writing center discipline claims to hold in its recent research and organizational discussions.

Chapter 4: Queer Writing Center Labor and/as Tension

Linked to distinct labor and to the guise of the progressive and queer-friendly field of higher education, chapter 4 discusses and analyzes moments of tension, violence, and oppression that stem from partici-pants' queer and administrative identities, arguing that tense instances distinctly impact work. In fact, the instances lead to forms of work themselves. Many participants still experience bullying, mobbing, micro-aggressions, and aggressions, even in seemingly progressive academe and even after acting as queer activist leaders who mentor and impact their institutional communities beyond their job descriptions. Such conversations about queer oppression are still necessary, despite disci-plinary stories of progress and assumptions of Left-leaning institutions and colleagues. While many participants discuss pairing their identity and their administration for varied forms of activism and advocacy, one participant, for example, reports being called the "fag professor," describing a culture of mobbing and bullying that impact his ability to mentor students and run his writing center to the best of his abilities. Another participant's supervisor mentions she cannot "technically" fire the participant for being a lesbian but does not assuage the participant's fears of termination or advocate for the participant to lead the center without fear of being out. This chapter does not simply seek to report complaints or oppressions but frames these perspectives within broader discussions of labor and administration in writing center administration.

Chapter 5: Conclusion

As a closing framework, I provide directive calls to action for writing center practitioners of all orientations—queer and nonqueer alike—to revisit and apply the study's central research questions. I also propel forward strategies for intentional recruitment and retention of queer administrators in the writing center world and for sustaining the disci-pline's proclaimed values, missions, and visions. The book closes with a cautionary but hopeful discussion about the long-term sustainability of writing centers as sites, methods, and practices. In closing, I also offer conversations about what nonqueer writing center practitioners might do with this book, as the book is, indeed, queerly focused. I frame these conversations in writing program administration, writing across the curriculum, and higher education studies in order to situate this book—one primarily about writing centers—in broader fields.

2

QUEER WRITING CENTER LABOR AND/AS CAPITAL

HISTORICAL VIGNETTES

Madeline describes "lesbian humor" as a rhetorical method she has used throughout her life. In her early life, as a young Girl Scout, she used humor to shed light on what she considered to be overly gendered practices in that organization. As a writing center director at research-intensive southern university, she still operationalizes "lesbian humor" regularly—sometimes to push back against heteronormativities she faces at her site, other times to exert queer power in redirecting administrative meetings in more productive and progressive directions. In fact, she regularly uses humor to stand up for those who can't stand up for themselves, she tells me, especially other queer people or people of color.

Brian expresses that a tough, queer, and Black administrative exterior—a demeanor he learned as a writing tutor at an HBCU (historically Black college or university) writing center—best suits his site and his administration. His mentor—also a Black writing center administrator—taught him that such temperament is what actually gets things done for Black students and tutors. His history runs counter to what he identifies as an identity-based administrative trope adopted by many of the field's queer white men—one that values nurturing personas, in particular.

Before coming to writing center work, Mike, now director at research-intensive university, was a grassroots AIDS organizer. He learned a lot in that world that would later help him in writing centers. Mike notes that nonjudgmentally meeting people where they are and helping them acquire agency in helping themselves are core ideas that immediately translated to tutoring writing during his graduate years. He also tells me, somewhat related to these organizing years, that a particular "readiness" (a term that will be taken up in this chapter) for interacting in the world as a queer person also informs his current writing center. The readiness may not translate to every instance of his leading his center or working with upper administration, but he says queer people are primed for reading audiences, reading rooms, reading situations, and reading safety to survive and thrive and everything in between.

DOI: 10.7330/9781646421497.c002

Writing centers are not Matt's first career. Before directing a high school writing center, he held positions in other industries. For Matt, this history, which he tells me gives him a tougher, more experienced exterior, has helped him push back against difficult upper administrations which, he says, may intimidate younger, first-career writing center practitioners. Matt's coming of age as a gay man taught him about what he calls "room-reading"— another framework discussed in this chapter. Matt says any room is a task in deciphering "friend or foe" as a queer person—for safety in being out has and continues to be a focal point for queer survival.

A writing center director in the South, John also grew up there. As a gay kid, he, like many queer people, found it was a difficult place to grow up gay and different. While he doesn't spend too much time talking about his upbringing, he praises the writing center field. He's impressed by the "more complex vision about writing center work," telling me his "being queer makes [him] more open and available to that conversation in the first place." When I ask him to unpack the statement, he tells me the South conditioned and instilled in him a hyperawareness of his surroundings, for better or for worse—something that mirrors and signals queer survival growing up in a homophobic culture and that complements his writing center work.

As a gay male writing center director, Ryan works the room, he tells me, playing on what he calls gay stereotypes to "get things done." He is convinced that many straight, white, and male colleagues bring a particular energy to academic spaces. His queer male energy is "less threatening" to his colleagues, especially his female ones, he says. He acknowledges these "soft" stereotypes, but having administered a successful, coastal writing center, he doesn't mind, as long as the work is done. He makes things happen, queerly, he tells me. Ryan believes gay men can administrate from a stance that runs counter to energy that often comes from straight male colleagues.

History matters. These opening vignettes showcase how participant histories tell us about the participants but also about how their histories connect to what this chapter calls *origins* and *capital*. The next sections will extensively define these terms and situate them in participant work. For brevity, however, *origins* are the embodied experiences and histories that these queer directors bring to their work and that particularly inform their work articulated in the book's later chapters focusing on activism and tension. *Capital,* for this book's purposes, is resources gained, lost, rendered, transacted, traded, and heralded in an institutional economy, whether embodied, material, or metaphorical, as related to one's social and economic standing. I draw from Pierre Bourdieu (1986) and writing center scholar R. Mark Hall (2010) to define this term in the next section.

Drawing from these stories, we in the writing center world all read and work rooms, know our audiences, and draw explicitly from our histories. But in the writing center discipline, do we talk about these moves, these histories, with the same attention as, say, our discipline's current focus on emotional labor? These historical vignettes teach us about what queer people initially bring to the administrative table of writing center work. Their histories afford them much and are complex beyond this book's introductory participant chart showcased in the introduction. As an extension of this book's introduction, which begins to complicate the writing center discipline's labor definitions, these queer participants teach us about what is necessary to survive and thrive within higher education.

Capital and identity are critical intersections for empirically tracing and better understanding labor in writing centers. Queer identity with a focus on capital offers nuance to such an intersection. At the moment, empirical writing center research often focuses on what writing center directors do and experience (Caswell, Grutsch McKinney, and Jackson 2016) and the work and site-based narratives we craft (Grutsch McKinney 2013), as this book examines. To be clear, such research is important and critical. Yet, in questioning such research-based directions, Neal Lerner (2019) describes the "turbulent state" of the writing center discipline despite a "semblance of success" in centers' on-paper missions (458) in his *College English* review of three recent book-length studies: *The Working Lives of New Writing Center Directors* (Caswell, Grutsch McKinney, and Jackson 2016), *Around the Texts of Writing Center Work: An Inquiry Based Approach to Tutor Education* (Hall 2017), and *Talk About Writing: The Tutoring Strategies of Experienced Writing Center Tutors* (Mackiewicz and Thompson 2018). From his examination of *Working Lives*, he argues that writing centers are plagued with literal and metaphorical "instability" resulting from the precarities of how they are staffed—often by non-tenure-stream faculty or staff—and of how they are framed in "temporary [research] concern[s]" instead of "research arc[s]" (459). In his closing remarks, Lerner expresses two primary concerns: referring to how *The Working Lives of New Writing Center Directors* interfaces with the relationship between disciplinary precarity and writing center work, individual administrations, and institutional support (461), he is "hard-pressed" to "solve the instability [the researchers] describe," despite his agreement with the book's conclusions. Further, while hopeful about how *Around the Texts* and *Talk about Writing* create opportunities for writing centers to "engage in meaningful research" (463), he describes both texts as being rather "inward[ly] turned" (463).

In these, the researchers leave out discussions of tutor identity in crafting claims about tutor-focused research and work, Lerner argues.

Lerner's concerns—what to do about unstable labor landscapes and how we might engage identity more forcefully to sharpen empirical and theoretical research—surface in this chapter. I too am left perplexed, unsure about how we navigate our way through a discipline that frames itself within the work of haves and have nots (Lerner 2006) and that regularly understands itself as a space where self-teaching and a good attitude trump disciplinary knowledge and academic degrees. I am no less confused by erasures of identity-based discussions in writing center empirical research—a thread that has informed my desire to write a book that draws these two elements together. To answer Lerner's (2019) question of what to do with and how to act in response to empirical data on writing center labor in recent texts, I argue mere investigation into what we do is a necessary but is only a first step in the direction of propelling forward the writing center discipline. So that we're not "hard-pressed" to gauge the "instability" of the writing center field (461), we must know what we bring to the table in the first place, especially through what this chapter calls *capital.*

In a discipline in which there's more work than we can possibly do (Caswell, Grutsch McKinney, and Jackson 2016) and in which field leaders call for more regular research for the long-term sustainability of our discipline, our sites, and our professional lives (Geller and Denny 2013), a focus on the acquisition of cultural capital is a necessary direction for our work, which is to say that the queer labor of this book is about a queer cultural capital and its acquisition in order to survive and thrive within writing center administration in higher education. Participants devise tactics, operationalizing their identities, if not sometimes flying under the radar strategically when they can (albeit some cannot fly under the radar). Participants, from their origins as queer people who are often oppressed, read rooms to survive but also to thrive. They work rooms, as Ryan does in this chapter's opening vignettes, understanding how and when to collect on the affordances of their queerness. Their labor, then, is applying queer capital to acquire a queer administrative mindset within the tricky arena that is higher education.

CAPITAL IN WRITING CENTER ADMINISTRATION

In his oft-regarded and oft-translated "The Forms of Capital," Pierre Bourdieu (1986) claims that, within social landscapes, one must acquire capital in order to maneuver throughout and be afforded standing within a cultural system. Capital, for this book's purposes, is resources gained, lost, rendered, transacted, traded, and regarded highly in an institutional economy, whether embodied, material, or metaphorical, as related to one's social and economic standing. For Bourdieu, capital and labor are intertwined. In fact, capital, for him, is "accumulated labor" that, when operationalized by actors, agents, or collective entities, "enables them to appropriate social energy in the form of reified or living labor" (241). Bourdieu additionally suggests that capital falls into distinct and occasionally overlapping categories: economic, cultural, and social (242), "cultural" being institutionalized often through "educational qualifications," broadly defined, with "social" framed and reified through "social connections" and occasionally "titles" ("of nobility," for Bourdieu) (242). This book's queer administrators, however, may teach us, as practitioners, about our work and its worlds of acquisition and exchange. Cultural and social capital best align with the navigational requirements and capacities of any writing center director. Perhaps. In the writing center world, R. Mark Hall (2010), in his research on writing center and writing-across-the-curriculum partnerships, argues rightly that Bourdieu's definitions focus on the individual rather than the collective. Drawing from theorists other than Bourdieu, he prefers to situate capital as "giving and getting something in return," which speaks to a "reciprocal nature of social capital" (18–19). While my book offers individual participant perspectives, I also rely on Hall's, in addition to Bourdieu, simply because of the reciprocal nature of writing center work itself, which does focus on the individual while also valuing the pedagogical and the collective. The places where we, as writing center directors, do work, especially doing the kinds of work Grutsch McKinney (2013) names, whether writing, reading, researching, mentoring, consulting, advocating, scheduling, tutoring, meeting, talking, or worrying (1–2), are sites where capital is acquired, exchanged, utilized, and disbursed. A writing center director understands, navigates, and negotiates an identity-based capital on the job. An understanding of capital as ever enmeshed in our work is a testament to how we are well primed to navigate landscapes at once invigorating and exciting but sometimes also fraught and tricky, as institutions of higher education often are. We, as writing center directors, use and exchange this capital based on the intersectional body we inhabit, whether we consciously think to do it or not, whether our disciplinary conversations refer to it or not, which, at present, most do not. There is, in fact, a labor inherent in this capital. Queer directors negotiate their capital, quite queerly, while the capital itself may be labor, as these chapters delve into, but in this case, the acquisition and application of capital are also part of the labor.

In this book, as the next section examines, queer participants invoke an awareness of their social landscapes, all representing a unique way for queer leaders to have facility in those spaces. These participants acquire social and cultural capital and have learned how to use it for personal and political gain within their sites. They are primed for the work, and have acquired the capital necessary for the work, and can do the work of higher education in ways that point back to their queer origins and rhetorical readiness—terms to be expounded upon. A writing center director must modulate between the countless hats a director must wear in order to lead their center and must exhibit and operationalize an awareness of capital in order to do the work we regularly name and catalogue in our discipline. It is these participants' intersectional queerness, especially at it relates to their origins and readiness, that informs their administrative acquisition of capital. The origins and readiness discussed in the next section, in which participants draw from queer experiences—some tongue in cheek and light-hearted, others oppressive and regressive—that make up their writing center administration with queer nuance, are not without their complex labor (to call upon the previous chapter's terms).

QUEER ORIGINS AS CAPITAL—CAPITAL AS WRITING CENTER LABOR

This section traces relationships among participants' personal and political origins, their rhetorical readiness for their work (as it relates to these origins), and the capital those origins and readinesses hold within participants' labor landscapes—terms and relationships to be unpacked in this section. In this context, capital cannot be understood outside participants' origins. *Origins* indicate personal histories of where and how these queer directors first came to their writing center work, much like this chapter's opening historical vignettes. These queer participants note, as many writing center practitioners do, a "falling into writing center work," meaning they, depending on circumstance and career path, had a graduate assistantship in a writing center, took a tutor-training course, or found themselves in tutoring positions that led to an orientation and desire to continue in the profession as full-time professionals. Yet even beyond these familiar narratives, queer participants are ready for the work of writing center administrative labor—the labor of meeting people where they are, in true writing center pedagogy fashion, whether working with tutors, writers, or colleagues; working to understand how to build sites that do things in the world; or working to combat oppressors and oppression—all of which take place and are enacted from a queerly nuanced vantage point. Long before they held writing center directorships, many participants held queerly oriented professional and volunteer positions. We learn from this chapter's historical vignettes that Mike was a 1980s AIDS organizer, for example. Madeline, whom we meet later in this chapter, was a transgressive young Girl Scout, challenging gender dynamics and rejecting an established organization, while other participants name how their world navigation of the past inform their writing center directorships at present. Directing a high school writing center is Matt's third career. John grew up gay in the South. Brian's history as a queer Black tutor at an HBCU makes him part of the lineage of his former director, also a Black man, whose administrative philosophy departs notably from what Brian names as a white narrative for gay men directing centers. Ryan works rooms, while Mike and Matt also offer spatial metaphors of survival when historicizing their queer administrations. These kinds of early positions are not without consequence for these participants, for it is these origins that lead to applications to their writing center administrative labors. Origins in queer world navigation and later application and acquisition of this workplace capital is a form of work—a labor ever so prominent in participants' work lives, much like the everyday tasks examined in recent writing center labor research (Caswell, Grutsch McKinney, and Jackson 2016; Geller and Denny 2013; Grutsch McKinney 2013). The relationship this work has to writing center administration relies on the conclusion that early queer origins lead to the application and acquisition of becoming queer writing center directors whose work departs from the disciplinary norm, especially that of "emotional labor" (Caswell, Grutsch McKinney, and Jackson 2016).

Queer Origins, Rhetorical Readiness, and Haunting Labor

Mike tells me that, while rewarding, the work of activist organizing was trying, with little sense of regular accomplishment despite tireless commitment and endless hours. Writing center tutoring, however, the work he first took on while a graduate student seeking funding, was differently gratifying, yet reminiscent of the work of AIDS education. For Mike, writing center administration is similar to "activist work around HIV and AIDS, trying to figure out people's needs and meeting their needs where they are, rather than where we might necessarily think they should be." Mike's aptitude for activist organizing, despite the trying, exhausting, perhaps less immediately impactful work it was for him, is a form of capital that informs his current writing center work. However, pulling from and reflecting upon his life is laborious because of its link to a historical epidemic that killed and continues to maim, harm, and destroy through material repercussion and ideological violence and inaction. For Mike, the work of writing centers, especially administration, is perhaps a bit haunting, despite his impact on the discipline. Which is to say Mike's reflections on queer suffering, oppression, and violence from that era, as they relate queer writing center directors' harnessing of experience to administration, is exasperating labor that extends beyond the traditional framework that complicates the compartmentalization of our professional and personal lives. As a queer former writing center director myself, do I regularly draw on my personal life to make sense of writing center administration? Certainly. Are particular forms of memory, channeling, and application more trying than others? Most certainly. The showcasing and application of such labor is quite, well, laborious, sometimes in a chilling, exasperating way. Which is to say that this learned navigation—this rhetorical savvy and readiness—is not without its embodied, trying labor for queer writing center administrators. Mike tells me about a queer rhetorical "readiness" that frames his writing center administration.

> Do I think about LGBT issues or who I am when I try to win over this dean? Probably not. But I think there's a lot of how I've been honed as a thinker, as a writer, to sort of develop rhetorical readiness in almost anything that I do, to morph, to adapt, to play to the audience.

The "rhetorical readiness" Mike speaks of, which gestures to Cal Logue's (1981) rhetorical theories about abject oppression, is academically and institutionally situated. However, the readiness of which he speaks may link to his AIDS organizing years, where he was on the front lines of an epidemic. During that time, as chronicled and evidenced by the work of Western activism, little demonstrative action took place given the demographics (i.e., queer people, people of color, and intersections thereof) the syndrome initially impacted. That is, queer people were suffering, were at the center of the crisis, and thus governmental AIDS and HIV awareness, prevention, and treatment lay stagnant for a half-decade, while a conservative administration refused to acknowledge the state of affairs for queer and of color bodies. Gay men and people of color took the hit, and then-President Reagan did not utter the word "AIDS" until 1985 and then again in 1987 (White 2004), years after the onslaught that resulted in thousands of 1980s AIDS-related deaths in the United States alone. In this sense, survival, for Mike and others, is not metaphor, whether in his descriptions of work or in his life as an organizer and later writing center director. Mike felt the atrocities of queer violence and erasure that plagued the early AIDS years and experienced a nuanced yet distinctly trying time as a bullied faculty writing center director.

Drawing upon his former life as capital for his current one is not an offshoot of the work; it is work—work Mike feels he was prepared for—readied for—from his vantage point as a queer person. These origins and these moments of readiness afford Mike much in systems of higher education. His explicit harnessing of them affords him capital in the realm of writing centers, which is to say that here I am not merely describing his past-to-present labor but showcasing how his queer history informs his work and his aptitude for it, however trying that work might be. Queer capital comes with a cost, as the experiences themselves, while harnessed for work, are quite laborious in their application to administration. The experiences are part of the landscape, Mike tells me, continuing, "I don't think you can be a well-integrated gay person without having internalized a performed rhetorical readiness, like reading every situation and asking yourself, 'Can I be out here? Do I need to be careful?'" In a world that begets caution from queer people for things like safety and well-being, Mike is on to something here. Queer people must navigate the world through this lens, as historically marginalized people have done long before this century. Despite showcasing the many joys of being a queer writing center director, the theme of being careful and cautious still pervades this book. His origins, which beget a capital of haunting readiness, afford Mike much, despite his experiences with queer trauma and oppression.

Queer Capital and Reading the Room

Matt tells me that walking into a room is its own rhetorical interpretation when deciphering "friend or foe." He goes so far as to tell me that the work of a writing center directorship is often similar to the work of growing up in the world queer, reading a room often with attention to one's own safety in spaces. Here, he echoes Mike's sentiments about surveying, existing, and being ready for what may present itself, whether friend or foe, upon his queer body—a savvy that also links to survival and that he (Matt) takes with him to work in writing centers. Allusion to relationships between spatiality and violence pervades many participant stories. Nearly every historical vignette that opens this chapter alludes to a room, what happens in it, how to read it, and how to exist within it as a queer person. In particular, participants don't discuss "reading the room" without follow-up comments about how to thrive or survive in the literal or metaphorical spaces they speak of. It is history, it is origin, however trying, that affords that orientation to writing center work. We see this spatial awareness—this metacognitive survival work—with Matt. Matt did come out and come of age during a trying time in US history—the same years Mike grew up in. And like Mike, Matt's origins as a queer person reading a room speak to his history of experiences with implicit and explicit homophobia.

Ryan describes the labor of room reading, especially his ability to not only read a room but to work one as well. His queer body offers him advantages many straight, white men may not have, he tells me. He describes a queer finesse white queer men can often strategize with and capitalize on, especially when working with straight women who regularly come up against and combat straight, white, male discourses, ideologies, and embodiments, and especially in academia, where women of all intersections often experience gender discrimination. Gay white male academics are not always innocent when it comes to bad behavior toward women colleagues, nor are all straight white male academics misogynists, to be sure. But, as Ryan describes, gay men are often able to productively soften their professional presence in ways other men don't or won't. Such professional action often affords Ryan much in the form of employing listening, silence, turn-taking, and collaboration. He describes himself as "less threatening" in administrative spaces, especially through his leadership. When I ask him to expound, he tells me he believes his queer body and administrative approaches themselves are what are less threatening, so much so that he believes he can capitalize on queer stereotypes to "get things done" administratively. I agree with him and have capitalized on those stereotypes myself at varied institutions in writing center and writing-across-the-curriculum administration, including and especially at my current site and especially in my relationships with women-identified colleagues. There is a certain capital in being able to inhabit a queer male body that is at once gendered and less threatening to our colleagues through queer performance and embodiment. And yet this labor falls upon a queer body to make up for and counter the energy that straight, white, male colleagues may bring to the room.

Madeline, while more focused on humor, echoes similar sentiments, explaining a "rhetorical savvy" for compensating or operating queerly in ways others may not be able to. In this sense, Madeline suggests queer people may even have a "leg up" on nonqueer professional counterparts, noting that her own humor—what she deems a more collective "lesbian humor"—is "disarming" and "puts people at ease" on one hand; on the other, it seeks to push back, strategically read rooms, bring things to the table, and redirect unproductive conversations. She tells me that such savvy and such humor often coalesce in order to face queer and race issues head on. This savvy—this "room reading"—despite her privilege as a tenured, senior writing center scholar, affords her and her rooms much in space making for queer issues in writing centers and academia. While Mike and Matt had previous work and professional lives—Mike in organizing, Matt in another profession outside of academic administration and teaching—Madeline's origins hold insights into her queer administration. Always named the "gay girl," she was active in the 1970s Girl Scouts organization, knowing that much of her "queer leadership" (her term at present) would be how she would approach communities she was a part of later in life. She ultimately left the organization, dissatisfied with what was possible for girls in the organization at that time. She identified more with what the Boys Scouts were doing. She preferred outdoor tasks, such as camping, hiking, and what at the time were deemed more male-centered activities, whereas the Girl Scouts, at the time, focused on homemaking, Madeline tells me, activities that did not interest her. Reflectively and retrospectively, Madeline looks back at the experience to say that she knew then she would go on to work and transgress within her communities for the greater good, as she had tried to do in that environment by questioning why women couldn't participate in the same ways as men. Madeline, quite literally, even as a preteen, quit or "opted out" (Ruti 2017) strategically in a fashion similar to how the queer theory field has recently identified a rejection of success narratives that control and normalize queer and nonnormative bodies. In drawing upon such capital of opting out, she has used those experiences to make sense of, push back within, and advance within the writing center discipline.

This queer orientation to questioning the status quo at an early age ("opting out"), for Madeline, gave way to her writing center labor, wherein she has done her best, she notes, to encourage intentional action in the broader field in order to give way to localized action in individual writing center sites, which is to say an early acquisition of readiness for the world gives way to a writing center administrative readiness that mirrors Mike and Matt, in both sentiment and experience, reading a room and rejecting its metaphorical parameters. In this sense, however traumatic, participants' rhetorical readiness through their queer origins is again a capital for navigating their later writing center administration. For Madeline, sometimes that capital of readiness—of queer survival—is also bound up in "making people laugh" and diffusing situations or conversations that may be headed in unproductive, if not homophobic, directions (e.g., she tells me of instances in which her self-described privileges as a tenured faculty member have allowed her to shut down potentially homophobic workplace conversations, nipping them in the bud before they could be articulated and allowed to infiltrate conversations that would impact her and, especially, others). It is noteworthy to continue pinpointing the labor of these queer, rhetorical moves that invoke, persuade, dissuade, and deflect homophobic audiences and contexts. It is work to be a funny lesbian who counters low-key ignorance with humor, which is to say someone has to do this work, and it is often these queer practitioners. Queer people and people of color are, indeed, often implicitly required to take on additional work to make things happen at an institution. When these queer practitioners do this work—read rooms to survive and help others do the same; make people to laugh to diffuse a situation—this work is no less laborious than any other tasks of their job descriptions.

Queer Capital, Resistance, and Fearlessness

John expresses experience with such work implicitly. At first, he tells me his sexuality and his identity play little role in his writing center administration. In fact, in other chapters, he is the first to tell me he is resistant to the idea of a "gay writing center" or a "gay writing center director." He even politely resists some of my interview questions. Yet he tells me growing up gay in the South wasn't without its challenges, as he says in the chapter's opening vignettes. While his older brother, who is also gay and came out before him (to significant tension with regard to their parents and community), took the brunt of the familial and local tensions of coming out, he learned early on that being gay wasn't acceptable, he tells me. Upon reflection, while still resistant, John does communicate that being queer in the South made him "hyperaware of surroundings" and "speech" and "how [he moves] through the world," and he "[pays] attention to people with a certain intensity," all of which are dynamics that "[lend themselves] to writing center work," which is to say even the book's most resistant participant still made connections among queer identity, identity-based capital, and an early aptitude for orientations toward writing center administration. Trauma around growing up in the South as a queer person, and in this case coming of age with a potentially homophobic family unit, resulted in its own trying capital through queer readiness, yet it is a state couched in trauma and oppression. John, however resistant to describing a relationship between his sexual identity and his writing center administration, draws attention to the capital of being a queer person in a writing center directorship.

Like Mike and Matt, his work is linked to readiness and origins that may be trying, if not traumatic. Yet, these participants prevail, do the work, and operationalize their origins, which is to say queer participants may push right through such traumatic occasions (Madeline tells me, especially in later chapters, that she "rolls right over" moments of homophobic tension in the workplace, disabling any caustic remarks directed at her lesbian identity. "I'm not afraid of anything," she says.). Having been introduced to a world we have to "roll right over" at early ages, to use Madeline's words, means labor in and stemming from implicit and explicit homophobia writing center administration is, essentially, not the challenge that, say, facing a homophobic family or culture is, but it does mirror the work of operationalizing trauma to do things in the world for the better. For these participants, long before they were writing center directors, they were people primed for its work with a thick skin. I say this because writing center work is hard, and higher education is often homophobic (as a later chapter explains). And yet these queer directors move through these spaces with savvy and suavity despite the trying nature of readiness-framed embodied capital. How can they not? And what challenge is writing center labor in a broader culture where queer people grew up having to make regular rhetorical decisions about survival (e.g., reading rooms, navigating coming out to and existing alongside homophobic families, "rolling right over" homophobia when appropriate and possible).

Queer Capital, Unicorn Status, and Reflections on Queer Pain and Survival
By this point in the book, I position queer writing center administrators as paradoxical unicorns, mythical creatures of their universities (said tongue in cheek) who check diversity boxes, read rooms, speak truths, protect the silenced, and soften spaces, representing an administrative phenomenon of being cast as a mythical, if not "perfect," seemingly rare representation of diversity but often white and able to pass enough to be perceived as recognizable, benign, and sometimes easily malleable (read: manipulated), and yet they are still bullied within heteronormative institutions. Certainly, these queer administrators mess up, they have bad days, they make bad decisions, and they face trial or tribulation that accompanies any writing center administrative position. And certainly not all queer people are equipped, ready, and suited for writing center labor; not even all the book's participants access, draw upon, and harness capital in the same ways. Many of the participants' perspectives are steeped in white privilege, with just two perspectives of queer people of color and one transgender perspective—subject positions

that complicate the relationship among origins, readiness, labor, and capital, as articulated in the next section. And arguably, we as writing center administrators all read rooms in ways Mike, Madeline, Matt, Ryan, and John do. Effective administrators are savvy and ready for the work, to use this chapter's terms. Recent research on labor shows us that despite a labor landscape where there's more work than writing center laborers can possibly do, most of us are trained for work and know how to seek disciplinary resources to get equipped for it (Caswell, Grutsch McKinney, and Jackson 2016, 171–74). In fact, those of us trained in the rhetoric and composition discipline are often quite audience aware and rhetorically savvy in our administrative approaches, our professional writing, and our interactions with colleagues as we represent and advocate for our writing-based sites, whether writing centers, writing programs, or writing-across-the-curriculum initiatives.

Yet, for queer people, people of color, and those in whom these identities intersect, this room reading, this savviness, this readiness is also always, perhaps, a coping strategy in the face of challenges unique to and nuanced by their work. In some cases, like Mike's, the inclination toward writing center administration is survival in hostile environments—what he calls in a later chapter "scrappy dog syndrome" and all its implications for marginalized peoples' writing center administration and sites. In later chapters, Mike tells us he believes straight white male administrators are often protected from such labor by their privilege and vantage points—which Matt alludes to earlier in this chapter—which is to say that particular kinds of labor most intensively hit writing center administrators of marginalized difference, as continually argued throughout this book. Capital comes at and stems from a cost, so to speak, especially to those of intersectional marginalization.

Jackie Rhodes (Rhodes and Alexander 2019) suggests that pain and violence create nuanced experiences for queer people. In most cases, pain is operationalized into action for these participants. Said a different way, many reflect upon past and present pain as queer people, whether in past lives as organizers at historically traumatic times or as people trying to live and survive, quite literally, in a world that may pedestal and hate them simultaneously. Pain, sans violence, is what Rhodes (Rhodes and Alexander 2019) would call a space for growth, individually and collectively. This kind of pain does craft within participants a readiness for survival in the world. The participants in this book identify this pain along the lines of queer fatalities and epidemics, of scanning a room to decide whether they can exist within and survive it, of laughing through tension to reappropriate it, and of "working" a professional space to disable its heteronormative and misogynistic undertones. In this chapter, pain leads to strength and readiness. Origin, then, a key concept of this chapter, is grounded in pain. But the pain begets a productive readiness for survival—which could be why participants are ready-made for writing center activism, as documented and discussed in a later chapter.

These painful origins evoke and give birth to survival capital. The administrative labor of these queer directors, then, is never too far from the application of capital to their working lives, which indeed offers practitioners of all walks of life a nuanced glimpse into queer writing center directors' labor. Participants' patterns of action represent origins and readiness for survival that inform their administrative aptitudes, which is to say the ability to survive and application of one's survival as a queer person to one's work is its own labor. This capital-based nuance differs from that of straight counterparts, to be sure. Such work is what also sets apart these particular queer white participants from the Black queers of the next section, whose origins and literate practices depart based on their engrained survival tactics, which are intersectionally complex in their Black and queer identities. And while Black experience certainly entails these survival origins, this Black labor does not explicitly match or mirror the lived histories of this chapter's mostly white administrators, but it certainly rhymes, as Brian and James make us privy to in the next section.

COMPLICATING ORIGINS AND READINESS: BLACK QUEER CAPITAL

Brian was readied for writing center work by a Black male writing center director, his mentor and teacher, while he was an undergraduate tutor at an HBCU, years before he was a graduate tutor and assistant at a nationally renowned writing center. There, he was baffled by the predominantly white institution's (PWI) operational and administrative differences in comparison to the HBCU—a bewilderment traced by recent Black and queer writing center researchers who suggest PWI centers are just simply different kinds of institutional spaces in their missions, visions, pedagogies, and spatialities, wildly different from sites that serve primarily marginalized writers at universities (Faison 2019; Faison and Trevino 2017). Brian echoes this sentiment, explaining that he learned from his mentor that the tougher exterior of a male writing center director gets things done in the university on behalf of Black students. "That's not how I was taught that writing centers operate," he tells me of PWI writing center missions, namely how they are led, especially when run by "queer cisgender white men." I take this statement to reflect a lack of diversity in writing center administrative philosophies, especially philosophies beyond those most adopted by queer white male directors. As such, the "diversity unicorns" of the writing center world are often queer white men, who are supposedly more intelligible and "less threatening" than other diverse, raced bodies. These diversity unicorns are like Ryan, whom we hear from in the previous section. They are those who can use their queer white bodies in rooms without fear of being called "scary" because of their race, as Brian is, though certainly not all rooms are safe for queer workers, as articulated throughout this book. Work within HBCU writing centers departs from the work and pedagogy of what a "white cisgender queer" writing center director is and does, Brian tells me several times when we talk. In expanding this discussion, he speaks with a broad but effective stroke in discussing such embodied labor, telling me that the discipline, when engaging queerness, only really investigates white queer bodies at PWIs, whether tutors, students, or administrators. Blackness is erased, he tells me, and I agree.

Similarly, Brian's sentiment that he has always felt unwelcome and erased from mainstream writing center scholarship and its representation of labor corroborates such a claim. When juxtaposed with the "white" narratives of the "nurturing" writing center director, especially that of the nurturing gay white male director, he expresses disdain, if not annoyance, communicating that those queer and male tropes dominate much of what it means to be a writing center director in the broader field. Diverse administrative voices are silenced, he tells me, and I agree with him. All the International Writing Centers Association (IWCA) anti-racist reading groups (IWCA 2018) and all the justice-based and radical writing center research (Greenfield 2019) and brave space discussions (Hallman Martini and Webster 2017b) in the world can't quite make up for a recruitment and retention issue of raced bodies. Whereas participants in the previous section note a readiness grounded in the labor of survival, they also note a readiness for the work from their previous experiences, and even from their previous writing center experiences that they "fell into" due to matches between their passions and their eventual administrative positions. Brian's readiness narrative departs from this one: he was trained thoroughly and he leads a fabulous center, yet his transition from an HBCU to a PWI was quite jarring for him, speaking to the intensity of a lack of diversity in bodies, pedagogies, and administrations in the writing center world. From this experience, he is also dumbfounded that, at the time of our conversation, little to no writing center scholarship about HBCUs exists.

He tells me his intersectional identity—a Black queer man, a multilingual writer and speaker, a person who grew up in a country other than the United States—all inform his work, but it is not always his queer identity that affords him capital, which is a departure from the capital white participants describe in the previous section. Race complicates Brian's queer capital. Many participants name their queerness as central to their work in leading their sites. Brian describes complications in simply identifying his queerness as a central maneuver in working within his center. But his identity intersections and their links to his work, especially the relationship among his queerness, Blackness, and multilinguality, he tells me, are difficult to parse out. At one moment, his queer experiences may take precedence in their application to his work, but his Blackness and linguistic background often take over, especially when supporting queer tutors of color or when working with multilingual students in the writing center, which is to say white privilege may actually inform how many queer participants are quick to name their queerness as the primary vehicle—the ultimate capital—that best readies them for writing center leadership and labor. Kimberlé Crenshaw's (1991) intersectional methods for understanding individual and collective oppression offer a critical lens for such Black and queer writing center readiness and capital, which is to say that, for some participants, their queer identity is merely one of many oppressed identities that are operationalized and that surface in their leadership.

Higher education's struggle to support its most vulnerable students through admission, matriculation, access, and retention (Brown 2019) exerts an immense pressure on leaders of color in higher education, especially those whose intersectional identities complicate their already-marginalized identities. Brian's struggle to name the capital that best informs his leadership and his support of his staff and students speaks to his complex intersectional identity, which is to say this book's eighteen white participants may more readily link their queer bodies to their work and its affordances and implications in spaces of higher education than do those whose bodies are more intersectionally marginalized. Mike, aware of this privilege, notes, "Our peers of color obviously already signify before they enter a space so their rhetorical readiness plays out in a different way," showcasing an awareness even among queer white leaders that Black writing center leadership differs from their experience.

Another participant of color, James, understands working on behalf of, if not saving, others, especially young Black queer men, he tells me. While he does not name himself an activist on campus in the ways other participants do in this book, he tells me his university participation often extends beyond the normal administrative gestures of writing center administration. In fact, he allied with an on-campus Black male initiative, and he said he has much to tell young Black men entering college—study hard, certainly—but he goes on to say he hypothetically would tell and literally has told young Black male college students, especially queer ones, not to bareback—or to have unprotected sex, that is. Jonathan Alexander (2008) teaches us that sexual literacies are oft-disregarded literate practices, hushed away in normative straight discourses, despite a Western culture that operates on and is quite enamored of sex and sexuality. James is viscerally aware of how his writing center directorship acts as a sexually literate vehicle, not so much for his own survival but for others' survival. Young Black queer men are among the most likely to contract HIV for a host of reasons grounded in access, education, and oppression (Centers for Disease Control 2019a, 2019b). James's origins as a queer Black man comingle with various chapter themes of labor, readiness, and capital in that his work has the potential for saving lives and is grounded in an understanding of the world from his own experience of rhetorical readiness and Black queer survival. The work of these Black queer administrators departs from this chapter's white capital labor articulated in the previous section. In particular, Brian and James focus on students, particularly students of color, queer students, and multilingual students. I am certain this chapter's white administrators care about students; however, their perspectives tend to broadly frame their administration in terms of colleagues' perceptions of their work, combating literal and metaphorical homophobia, and the discussions of room reading of the previous section. But for Brian and for James, a tough exterior and hard conversations (about safe sex) tend to do more for Black and queer students, it seems. They corroborate such a claim explicitly, telling me that working on behalf of Black students is about these two approaches: being tough and talking about tough things. However, it is also interesting what stories they opt to tell when asked. White capital tends to be narrated more abstractly in "rooms," whereas Black capital lives concretely in direct student impact. Such a reality may point to the position types of these administrators—both practitioners work quite extensively with students (they are directors whose job descriptions require them to tutor, whereas some project participants do not directly tutor students). And later chapters, especially this book's activism chapter, teach us queer directors tend to look out for, protect, stand up for, and even "save" queer and nonqueer tutors. Black queer writing center capital also often informs similar work.

However trying, harnessing this knowledge base—this lived experience as a queer man of color—affords James capital in his administration in that he uses his writing center administration and leadership to change Black narratives and to prospectively save Black queer lives. His admitting that he has and will continue to tell young queer Black men to protect their sexual health, he reveals that his origins—his own readiness for his own previous and present survival—are part of his labor and leadership landscape, for which a trying capital is ever present. The realities of queer people's work are never too far from their origins of survival during trying times. James tells me about this part of his leadership rather matter of factly, as many participants who engage with sexual-health initiatives through their writing center leadership do (more of this conversation surfaces in this book's activism chapter). In this sense, James's Black and queer body affords him, his site, and his leadership the capacities—the capital harnessed from his own origins and readiness for writing center leadership—for making change and propelling forward Black queer survival.

TOWARD CHAPTER 2 AND ACTIVISM IN WRITING CENTER WORK: LABOR, CAPITAL, AND SEXUAL- AND MENTAL-HEALTH ADVOCACY

James's activism around sexual health impacts this project, first in that writing center-labor scholarship has not yet delved into the relationship among sex, sexual advocacy, sexual health, and writing center labor and administration. Queer peoples' relationship to their sexual and mental health is paramount to their lived experiences. In reality, queer people must navigate a world that is at once oppressive, regressive, and progressive, which takes a toll on queer sexual and mental health, a claim corroborated by national depression and suicide rates for queer people (National Alliance on Mental Illness n.d.), as well by the realities of historic homophobia and transphobia in medical institutions. Participants understand such dynamics. In later chapters, participants Dana and Casey teach us that being a queer person is often understanding one's relationship to mental health, sex, and sexuality, alongside global cultures that may, on one hand, pedestal queer bodies and on the other shun and enact violence upon them. To be a queer person, then, is to exhibit certainly an origin and a readiness for understanding and coping with one's own sexual and mental health in an unstable global landscape. Further, being a queer or transgender person is also being an advocate for one's and others' sexual health, per medical institutions that have historically erased and enacted violence on queer and raced bodies. In such a regard, Dana explains that not every aspect of her writing center leadership is necessarily a queer moment but may afford her and other stakeholders a queer slant of sorts. It is important to note that, like many participants, she reports being the "go-to" person for all things queer, along with any sticky, trying, or traumatic experiences that impact tutors' lives—a state of being that arises and will be unpacked later, especially in this book's activism chapter. In the ways Mike explains queer rhetorical readiness for queer life in the world writ large and for writing center leadership, Dana's sentiments point to moments in which she is the go-to person if, for example, a student or tutor is "raped on campus." And, because of her outness about her own mental health, she finds that tutors regularly consult her about their mental health, whether about depression or suicide.

Many other participants note such instances. It is their queerness and outness that creates a line at their office door for the performance of this labor. The next chapter, in fact, starts with discussions of condoms and dental dams and of suicide support and depression discussions as forms of activism. For example, because his institution does not have a campus health center, Tim houses condoms in his writing center. They ought to be available to students somewhere, he tells me. Cara expresses a similar sentiment about her site but advocates for the availability of dental dams through her center's relationship with women's and lesbian organizations on campus. Casey tells us that helping a transgender tutor through suicidal ideation and through resource access and identification is some of the most important work she will ever do in her life, much less in a writing center directorship. A transgender writing center director, Jack advocates for crafting writing spaces that humanize queer and transgender bodies in order to save queer and trans lives, he tells me. When participating as a transgender voice in a gay-straight alliance at his institution, he hopes his presence and voice as a writing center director and leader offer nonqueer, if not transphobic, audiences a vehicle for better understanding and supporting trans voices. He tells me that if his body can "teach" colleagues about transgender perspectives, that education may lead to one less transgender suicide in the grand scheme. Above, James describes telling young queer men at a writing center partnership event not to bareback; all of these instances point back to an awareness of the complexity of queer directors' work lives.

These queer practitioners have often experienced the very things they're advising and supporting students through, whether suicidal ideation or attempts, sexual and raced discrimination from medical sites, or experiences that spoke to needs for sexual-health initiatives. If

the personal is the political, these writing center practitioners understand that mantra with compassion and proactivity. These are vulnerable moments that participants describe, yet these directors afford
stakeholders and landscapes much through their queer leadership. By
maintaining that each situation points to capital in sexual and mental
vulnerability, I do not intend to undermine or inscribe flippancy on
these instances by merely identifying them as capital, which may imply
a capitalism or a mere denominational exchange, as if human emotion,
its embodiment and its impact, is merely a study in capitalism, revenue,
exchange, and the whole bag. Instead, the focus here on capital is
about what's possible in writing center leadership when queer people
lead, when they reflect, and when they apply their origins and readiness
to their work—essentially, a focus on what queer administrators bring
to the table. What we, as practitioners, can learn from these queers
is the possibility of applying our humanity to our work, perhaps even
when that humanity is traumatic and trying, fraught with promise and
peril. It is important to understand the framework of origins and readiness for such work exhibited by these queer directors how they apply,
understand, and advocate from their sites by relying on their histories.
Queer leaders' origin, readiness, and capital affords a complex—and
complicated—disciplinary glimpse that could inform how we, as writing
center practitioners of all orientations, take up current directions in
writing center work.

CONCLUSION

Negotiation of intersectional queer capital is part of
queer writing center labor . . .

In this chapter, capital is framed in queer origins and readiness from
one's past and personal life. Participants' origins and readiness are
queerly harnessed within labor landscapes but were no less laborious
themselves, which is to say that operationalizing one's origins and readiness capital (i.e., the reflection, acquisition, and especially application)
is its own labor, to be sure. This capital is costly for queer participants,
as this chapter's trying stories point to a beautiful but traumatic tension
between being a queer writing center worker and fusing their origins,
readiness, and capital with working life. A preparedness based in an
intersectional identity is a survival and coping asset in higher education.
Such realities, however, point to a landscape in higher education that
leaves much to be desired if survival is a navigational framework for a professional, queer or otherwise, understanding their place within a system.

Raced intersections complicate this conversation. White participants feel that they adequately "fell into" writing center administration with a strong local and disciplinary support system, meaning they were prepared to work in the writing center discipline. A course or a mentor offered them a foundation that offered them local success in navigating writing center administration at their sites. Black participants note such readiness, too. Further, most of this chapter's participants showcase connections among their bodies, their origins and histories, their capital, and their labor. White perspectives showcase privilege in that white participants also report holding up a mirror to the writing center discipline and seeing "themselves" and their capital in the reflection, whether in leaders, in research, in pedagogies, or in visible administrative orientations that guide our field. Black participants—Brian, in particular—do not feel HBCU writing center praxis nor Black administrators are adequately reflected in mainstream writing center praxis—a reality that especially teaches us about a lack of representation of Black writing center praxis.

. . . But capital isn't merely a queer administrative concept.

This reality has implications and lessons for queer and nonqueer writing center directors. At the moment, we talk a lot about our writing center labor, as it intersects with present conversations in higher education whether we're talking about presidential and upper-administrative salaries, federal funding, contingent labor, or practitioner, site, or disciplinary sustainability in a national arena, where higher education is certainly under attack. One only needs to look to former President Trump's appointment of a Secretary of Education, Betsy DeVos, who didn't have a background in teaching, public education, or, well, anything that would justify ascending to such a position. In this macro-case, the system was being set up, ultimately, to fail and to be directed away from an educated populace with local and global access and resources to become and stay educated. Higher education's discussion of and fixation on labor is a vehicle for making sense of and making plans for a shifting landscape in which we are laborers. The writing center discipline is not immune to such realities, nor is any practitioner leading a writing center site. A focus on embodied capital, or at the very least upon how we do our labor and harness our bodies for particular outcomes, is critical. These queer practitioners afford writing center leaders, queer and nonqueer alike, much in the way of complexity to this critical conversation of working and existing in higher education at the current political moment. In this sense, analyzing catalogues of our work, as current writing center research does, is critical (Caswell,

Grutsch McKinney, and Jackson 2016). The next step in that direction, as this chapter argues, is to also understand the nuances of that labor, especially how our bodies and our histories ready us for doing our work and making change, which is to say that . . .

Writing center research doesn't yet account for capital, at least identified in that way.

When we talk about our work empirically, we tend to list it, to case study it, and to frame it as impossibly difficult to do, complete, and thrive within. And to be sure, writing center work is certainly all of that. Catalogues and case studies hold strong rhetorical weight for framing our discipline's understanding of labor. But these are starting points. When juxtaposed with this book's queer perspectives, a key and current term, *emotional labor,* alongside its sister research frameworks for describing labor—everyday and disciplinary (Caswell, Grutsch McKinney, and Jackson 2016)—need further applicable frameworks, not only because the queer perspectives from our field's diverse practitioners do not adequately coalesce with these definitions but also because little conversation exists about writing center origins and capacities for work or about how labor is enacted and performed by bodies, queer and non-queer alike.

PARTING WORDS TO ACTIVISM

Capital—alongside this book's sister frameworks of activism and tension in later chapters—teaches us, as writing center practitioners of all orientations, about our work. Participants showcase the trickiness of writing center administrative work with its all-too-familiar rewards, which converse (sometimes with tension, a focus of a later chapter) with the discipline's rightful fixation on actively building writing centers that do things in the world (often beyond tutoring and the decided-upon-but-ever-shifting work of writing centers). The next chapter showcases how these origins and capital lead to capacities for pressures alongside directors to use their writing centers to do things—things that often look, feel, and embody activism and advocacy for people and causes not immediately associated with writing center work. According to participants, this work is somewhere between a beautiful possibility, "a calling" of sorts, and a trying, sometimes exhausting labor that impacts other individual, local, and disciplinary work.

In continuing to map this book's trajectory, not too distant from chapter 3's activist labor conversations are participants' tensions discussed in chapter 4, which teach us about the realities of bullying, mobbing, erasure (in the discipline, often), and the tumultuous national landscape. Such realities impact work, but they are also forms of work, as is continually argued throughout this book. Such tensions are intertwined with this chapter's discussion of oft-trying capital, which, like activism and tensions, makes way for impactful queer orientations to on-the-job labor. But like other chapter themes, capital is its own labor, for acquisition and application of rhetorical readiness is, indeed, writing center work, as participants describe in this book's two forthcoming chapters.

3
QUEER WRITING CENTER LABOR AND/AS ACTIVISM

HISTORICAL VIGNETTES

Tim is a faculty writing center director at a midwestern regional compre-
hensive. He has fostered his visibility carefully on campus, as he founded
the LGBTQA faculty committee and coleads campus-climate conversations.
Upon his arrival, Tim realized his institution did not have a health center
that would actively acknowledge World AIDS Day. His center responded to
student needs by hosting a World AIDS Day event. That day, he and his
staff stocked the writing center with condoms for both student access and
university awareness. The distribution of condoms in his center is a prac-
tice still in place today.

A queer Black man, James orients to his work from a full-time, staff-level
position, where he has worked for several years. He is an accomplished
writer who also teaches, and he found his way into writing center work
because of its intersections with his own professional life and desires. His
institution is an urban site that serves an exponentially growing number
of students of color—Black young men in particular. He sees his site as
one that helps writers with writing, first and foremost. When we talk about
his center's work and outreach, however, he tells me that he is active in his
site's Black Male Initiative and that he has opportunities, as the writing
center director, to speak and influence Black males. In thinking ahead
about his forthcoming workshop, he tells me he would revel in the oppor-
tunity to speak with young queer Black men about safe sex. He would tell
them not to bareback, or have unprotected sex, for example.

A transgender man, Jack transitioned while working at his current writing
center. He struggled many years before transitioning but has been met with
professional support as his site's director. Writing center work and research,
he tells me, have always been meaningful to him in relationship to his
identity as a transgender person. His work environment, where he holds a
secure, staff-level position in a rural area, is certainly not perfect, however.
He has been asked to serve on LGBTQA panels with varying levels of suc-
cess. He speaks his truth on those panels. He does so because he believes his

DOI: 10.7330/9781646421497.c003

story may have positive impact in the world, especially in his local area. He thinks about transgender suicides and how his body and his story may help transform the grim realities of what it means to be a transgender person during the Trump administration.

Cara is out and proud in her writing center at a research-intensive mid-western university. At the time of this study, she held a secure non-tenure-track faculty position and an executive-level directorship. She identifies her queer and lesbian identities as comingled with her writing center administration, mission, and vision. She teaches her tutor-training courses with queer activist scholarship in mind. She tells me her southern upbringing and her few years in the closet in her youth impacted her coming out. Her focus on visibility and transparency link, in many ways, back to a story she tells me. In the late 1980s, a former high school classmate of hers passed away of AIDS. He came home to die with friends and family in the South, but his parents kept his sexuality and his condition under wraps. He died before she and others got the chance to say goodbye and without anyone knowing he had AIDS. This erasure impacted how she thinks about the positive impact of queer visibility, voice, and activism in her writing center.

Writing center work is complex, ever enveloped in the ways these queer and trans perspectives orient these directors to how they labor on behalf of their sites, their tutors, and their students. Stemming from the last chapter's discussion of the labor of embodied history, readiness, and capital, the work of this chapter deals with condoms, dental dams, LGBTQA parade marches, promoting sexual- and mental-health initiatives, and "calling [people] out on their shit" (but "politely," says a participant), leading us, as practitioners, into relatively uncharted writing center research territory. Such work is distinct, nuanced, and could even be cause for discomfort for the readers of this book. All participants in this study note an orientation, if not a responsibility, to use their writing center administration to do more than just offer student writing support. The support is often, but not always, queerly focused, or geared to the support of queer initiatives or people. Whether mentoring, supporting, and consoling queer and nonqueer tutors, hosting queer-focused events, or holding space for sexual- and mental-health support in their centers, participants name regular, intentional administrative approaches that step outside our disciplinary administrative orthodoxies. This chapter examines what this kind of queer writing center work—this activism—looks like and how it is named by participants. It further claims queer directors are differentially positioned and expected to do such labor, with glimpses into the individual and collective implications of such work, especially how the work extends beyond conventional writing center labor.

National and international writing center organizations and publication venues encourage a certain orientation to labor through activism and advocacy. The current political climate certainly calls for such site-based activism and advocacy, especially in an age where writing and rhetorical education are implicitly and explicitly under attack (think "fake news"). Queer writing center leaders are often at the center of such conversations. In 2010, for example, Denny (2010) called attention to the silences surrounding the case of Tyler Clementi, an undergraduate who committed suicide after being outed publicly by his roommate (Rose 2010). From Denny's lead, other writing center scholars chimed in (Sloan 2010), noting disciplinary silence on the writing center listserv and the field at large. These events and their disciplinary responses might seem dated, given 2018 discussions on the writing program administration listserv (WPA-L) that stemmed from Michelle LaFrance's (2018) initial crowd-sourcing of rubrics, which ended with a calling out of varied forms of "mansplaining" as they intersected with gender, race, class, sexuality, and institutional status. Yet, from such past and present disciplinary moments, calls for alliance and participation have arisen, especially noting, as Denny (2010) and Sloan (2010) in the writing center world have, that silences offer their own disciplinary arguments.

Writing center research lends itself to a certain activism, as explicated in recent studies. Grimm (1999) and Grutsch McKinney (2013) do not offer explicitly queer or traditionally activist texts, yet their encouragement to understand postmodernity and to recognize and retell stories, respectively, point to historic traditions of queer activisms. Much of what is understood through the lens of queer theory—a subfield of critical theory that arose in academia from 1960s Black, women's, and queer movements—is about disruptions to modernity and grand narratives, which are core concepts of Grimm's and Grutsch McKinney's work. In the writing center world, Denny (2011) calls our field to consider how attention to identity intersections allows practitioners to understand, navigate, and subvert oppressive forces, often institutionally. Greenfield's (2019) recent advocacy for a new writing center paradigm grounded in love shifts conversations away from a primarily student writing support model to creating sites that radically face and denounce oppression. Denny's and Greenfield's core arguments suggest that such activism and advocacy do and ought to exist within our work. Other notable calls for writing center activism ask practitioners to consider bravery over safe spaces for our sites (Hallman Martini and Webster

2017b); to examine how queer theories and orientations impact writing center spaces and pedagogies (Denny 2005, 2011; Doucette 2011); to understand the impact of systemic and institutional racism upon writing centers (Green 2018; Faison et al. 2019; Greenfield and Rowan 2011; Riddick and Hooker 2019); to define parameters for embodied writing center activist responses (Diab et al. 2012; Goins and Heard 2012; Lockett 2019; Ozias and Godbee 2011; Smith 2012); to call forth alliance and accomplicing in writing center work (Green 2018); to queer and diversify our writing center research methods (Lockett 2019; Simpkins and Schwarz 2015); to call forth intersectional stories of race, sexuality, and class (Condon and Olsen 2016; Faison and Trevino 2017); to queer our everyday and administrative writing center practices (Dixon 2017); and to listen to stories that offer identity-based nuance to counter claims that writing centers are only ever just sites of writing support (Denny et al. 2019). Further, the 2018 International Writing Centers Association (IWCA) Conference, "The Citizen Center" (IWCA 2018), was organized around the themes of social justice, equity, and access; the conference hosts encouraged practitioners to consider the implications for writing center sites and labor of attention to social justice, while many regional conferences have also taken up comparable themes and issued progressive calls for proposals (CFPs).

We, as researcher-practitioners, ought to be taking up these CFPs. Dana, a participant, notes "[validation]" in seeing so many "CFPs that have emerged [about social justice] and IWCA's position statement on the singular they." The conversations about social justice in the writing field and its mother and sister disciplines are so prevalent that it's glaringly noticeable when the efforts in the field do not account for the realities of how our work intersects with macro- and microactivisms. For example, the above-mentioned 2018 IWCA "Citizen Center" CFP, with its entire conference program and activities linked to varied forms of intersectional activisms, starkly contrasts with the 2019 IWCA CFP, which did not engage with justice and identity and which was framed in the scholarship of a white, straight, male scholar. I do not point this out to critique or shame the organizers of the 2019 conference but to showcase just how much social justice, activist, and queer lenses have shaped our work, at least at face value, in the past decade. Still, a notable critique from Rebecca Hallman Martini (2018) is that writing center theories that posit activism are well intentioned but perhaps are merely following disciplinary trends, not doing the actual, hard work of activism. By extension, her critique allows me to consider carefully what queer activist writing center work looks like and who is asked to do this work and to lead in the discipline. An answer lies in this chapter.

Activism is tricky to define. In popular culture, *activism* aligns with tropes of organizing, marching, and vocalizing against oppressive ideologies and institutions. In the gay world, we might note June Pride celebrations, dating back to the 1969 Stonewall riots that signaled gay rights movements when transgender and queer people of color fought back against ongoing police raids of New York City's Stonewall Bar. We might also note the 1970s activist work by transgender people of color (e.g., Marsha P. Johnson and Sylvia Rivera), or 1980s AIDS Coalition to Unleash Power (ACT-UP) activism. Despite dominant cultural narratives, activism is many things for many people. For this chapter, I define queer writing center activism as administrative labor that exceeds the conventions of writing center work articulated in earlier chapters (especially the conventions Grutsch McKinney [2013] opens *Peripheral Visions for Writing Centers* with) and that attempts, explicitly or implicitly, to enact social change in general or to signal progress in lived material queer conditions, whether local, institutional, disciplinary, or global. I understand some may see the work of the participants in this study as bordering on advocacy over activism, and I can understand such claims. However, activism and advocacy are difficult to parse out, even for people deeply entrenched in such work. A common distinction is that activism works outside of institutions and reflects direct, explicit attempts toward change, resolve, or revolution, while advocacy entails working with an institution in more indirect, subversive ways. I can understand this supposed distinction, but I struggle, for example, to identify how this chapter's participant stories fit neatly within either such category. For example, participants are certainly doing things in their writing centers that are direct and indirect action, explicit and implicit work. Further, I disagree with the stance that activism only takes place "in the streets" (i.e., outside dominant institutions, such as universities) alongside traditional historic tropes (e.g., marching and protesting), which is to say I acknowledge this distinction and also prefer to yield to the word and framework of *activism* in this chapter and throughout this book.

WRITING CENTERS AS DE FACTO ACTIVIST SITES
FOR SEXUAL HEALTH AND AWARENESS

Tim and his tutoring staff step up where the university can't and won't. His writing center has become a place—the only campus space, in fact—where students can access sexual-health resources. Early in his tenure, he housed condoms in his writing center, initially as a response to an AIDS Day event but later as a permanent fixture. He tells me his center houses these resources because other offices on his campus don't. At the time of this study, there was not a health center nor sexual-health resources on campus. He told me, "There was no place for those condoms to go, so we've had condoms in the writing center ever since, which gets weird looks sometimes. I don't know where else to put them [on campus], but I want them to be somewhere." They need to go somewhere. Such a comment points to necessity.

In this vein, Cara notes that writing center directorships often allow for control over a space, a rarity in university environments. Such spatial control has allowed her at her current and previous universities to make room for diverse, often queer, voices and activities. She reflects on her previous site, where she was appointed a Lambda faculty advisor. She notes, laughingly, that the site's Lambda Organization may have recruited her for a faculty advisor position not for her queer identity but for her writing center space. She explains,

> They were having issues with meeting space and them having not only space that they could use but having a regular space helped them have an identity for students and helped students kind of know where to find them and find us. Being able to offer that space up to the Lambda group and be there consistently and having an office where they could store materials or whatever. Back then, we didn't go so far as to have the bowl of condoms and dental dams in the writing center. I probably would do that now if I was the Lambda advisor.

Cara echoes Tim's concerns about universities making space or resources on sexual-health offering her space as one such site.

Writing center directors often do work well beyond their job duties, yet here queer directors move into uncharted territory that exceeds the historic conventions of our labor (Grutsch McKinney 2013). It is noteworthy, furthermore, that Tim's center's condom availability indeed takes place not in a writing center on a seemingly liberal coast but in a well-established center at a midwestern regional comprehensive. Cara, while now a faculty director at a major midwestern research site, tells a story that took place in the rural south. These participant perspectives challenge many disciplinary and cultural assumptions about where writing center justice work takes place, namely the perception that activism only takes place on the coasts, or the conception that such work only takes place at research institutions like Cara's, yet Tim's regional comprehensive writing center is responding to the politics of sexual health with rigor. But there we have it: condoms and dental dams in the writing center, with queer people leading the way through distinct, nuanced work. Such work is quite invisible as well. Perhaps condoms are material objects, but such sexual-health advocacy is quite invisible and difficult to name and translate for a job description or annual review, for example. Further, such work is not necessarily emotional labor as it plays out in the field's recent, award-winning case studies (Caswell, Grutsch McKinney, and Jackson 2016), despite an emotional component and capacity for the work. I say this because the work these queer bodies are doing far exceed our field's definitions for emotional labor, which rely primarily on emotional components and situational mediation. A queer body in a writing center space doing this kind of queer work (e.g., sexual-health advocacy) is its own kind of labor and is often specific to its queer laborer.

A man of color, James tells me his institution is mostly made up of adult learners, but with the emergence of a younger admitted demographic, his school now has a Black Male Student Success Initiative, which he was asked to support. Asked to speak to a group of young Black men, he felt initial discomfort that we heard in this chapter's opening vignettes:

> I'm like, these brothers, are they gonna be okay with me being out, how out can I be? I didn't speak to them directly about being openly gay. I suspected that maybe one or two of them were gay. But I was just talking about the importance of the stuff I always say: "You need to read all the time. You need to go to the writing center. You can do it. I did it, and I got kicked out. I went back and I got a doctorate." That kind of stuff, so, but I would love to do that. I would love to talk to them about sexuality, keeping yourself safe, don't go around bare backing with guys you don't know and stuff like that. I would love the opportunity to talk about that to them about that kind of thing.

A safe-space representative himself in addition to his writing center directorship for his campus, he notes further sexually driven activist discussions. He tells me, "Any interested faculty and staff, they come and we talk about this broad spectrum of the queer community. You may have heard some of this language. You may be curious. How can you help students when they come to you with various issues that they have around being LGBT. This is the lingo so we're like, this is the glossary of terms you should know. These are the different types of sexuality. You thought there was just gay and straight. Sit down. We're gonna educate you about sapiosexual, this and this and this and this and so it's an eye-opener for them. On my door here I have a safe-space sticker so people know. It was left over from the previous writing center coordinator and I said that stays, not going anywhere. I hope that students recognize that this is a place where they can come and feel free to talk to me about those things."

Cara and Tim hold tenured positions in established midwestern writing centers and arguably may be perceived as having the luxury to promote sexual health at their sites. In this sense, the notion of the academic freedom of two established administrator-scholars who offer up their sites as social justice ones may lead us to believe this situation is merely institutional privilege speaking. Both are white and cisgender and report general acceptance of their identities and practices at their institutions. James, however, holds a full-time contingent administrative position at a community college, so his job security is presumably more precarious. Yet James's pause to reflect upon "what he would say" to young queer Black men about barebacking aligns with the administrative orientations of both Cara and Tim, despite his non-tenure-track position. James discloses no fear of being fired for his administrative orientations, nor for his work to build a writing center pedagogy that supports the sexual health of young Black men. James, and many others in this project, counter disciplinary lore that suggests writing center activism, especially queer activism, is only made possible by particular regions, particular institution types, and particular work-based privileges, such as tenure, promotion, and clout.

These three perspectives point to a responsibility. Tim explicitly acts as the sole person whose administrative site responds to sexual health, as his institution does not have a health center. He and his tutors are de facto purveyors of this knowledge and this action. The actions of Tim, Cara, and James have historic roots. Queer people have often had to act when others wouldn't. I make this claim with ACT UP in mind. Queer people have had to subversively manipulate the system to save the vulnerable and to save themselves. Queer writing center directors doing this work point to a history of queer people taking care of each other in the face of erasure that kills—erasure often linked to the relationship among sexual activity, shame, and a lack of resources, knowledge, and awareness. There is privilege in apathy, in inaction, which is to say James's orientation to telling young queer Black men not to bareback demonstrates his understanding his role as a writing center director—administrator of a site trusted at his institution, a claim supported by his invitation and presence at a Black Male Initiative—as an embodied platform for Black queer support. James's attention to barebacking, sans the cultural inclination to shame it, counters problematic claims that AIDS is an epidemic of "the past" (World Health

Organization n.d.), with specific attention to how transmission of sexual infections impacts queer communities of color exponentially more than white queer communities of privilege (Centers for Disease Control 2019a, 2019b). James may know that a culture in which privileged white gay men have access to PrEP[1] (HIV.gov) may inadvertently create dangerous landscapes for poor queer people of color, especially transgender people of color. Barebacking on or off PrEP may mean life or death for these queer men he seeks to care for. He rounds out this discussion by mentioning his office's safe-space sign—perhaps a metaphor for his understanding of the complexities of safe sexual practices in the twenty-first century.

At this point, readers may feel the need to poke at these participant perspectives, thinking, "I do that. Any director could or would do that work." There may even be raised eyebrows at condoms and dental dams being in writing centers. Practices like these were notable departure points in queer participants' activist labor. Queer people have trying histories with medical and psychiatric institutions and world health crises and epidemics, which have historically killed us over centuries. Death came from late nineteenth-century medical writing that rendered queer people psychologically damaged and gave rise to modern conceptions of conversion violence (Blakemore 2018). Death came from that same medical writing that described a homo/hetero binary (Katz 1995), a binary that later rendered erasure or pathology leading to a century of suicides or ignored medical epidemics. Death came from a June 5, 1981, Centers for Disease Control Morbidity and Mortality Weekly Report (2001) detailing five cases of mortality from *Pneumocystis carinii* pneumonia for five otherwise healthy Los Angeles gay men—a report that adumbrated thousands of deaths before medical or political stakeholders acted in favor of queer people. Death came from twenty-first-century demagoguery that willfully misrepresented transgender people, leading to an epidemic of transgender violence and fatality. Arguably, any director can put out condoms and dental dams in their writing centers, certainly. But to be sure, these queer directors do this work by living out and alongside an embodied history. In the 1980s, Cara's longtime high school friend who had long departed the South after graduation came home to die of AIDS, as discussed in this chapter's opening vignettes. She never got a chance to say goodbye, and his parents wouldn't name his ailment or allow him visitors. During the same time period, Mike, whom we heard from in chapter 2's opening and hear from again in later chapters, was a fearful but committed young AIDS organizer watching the horrors of what a "gay epidemic" could do to a community of queer men. So anyone can put out condoms in their writing center? Certainly. But does this embodied labor of memory mean something quite different for these queer directors? Most certainly.

Queer people historically have had to act because no one else would. To distribute condoms, to offer dental dams, to craft spaces where sexual health resources are front and center alongside tutoring and student support is, perhaps, a means for these directors to complicate the work of the writing center. I do not think this attention to sexual health ought to be the work of all writing centers, but I do think we must challenge the orthodoxies of our labor, recognizing that our work may not be easily parsed out—that radical work (Greenfield 2019) may be the work we must do and that queer people may feel a particular, nuanced responsibility for such labor based on this historic precedence. It is again notable that most of this work-based advocacy is relatively invisible labor, in terms of documentation in a work evaluation or curriculum vitae, for example.

PARTICIPANTS NAMING QUEER ADMINISTRATIVE IDENTITIES IN WRITING CENTERS

Many participants name work that links to this chapter's definition of queer activist writing center labor—that which exceeds the conventions of writing center work and that attempts, explicitly or implicitly, to enact social change or to signal progress for lived material queer conditions, whether local, institutional, disciplinary, or global. Yet several participants seek to draw distinct boundaries for their work; they tell me that their sites do quite intensive justice work while saying their site isn't the "gay writing center" or that their pedagogies only focus on practice. Countering James's attention to safe-space signs, John, for instance, will not display an LGBTQA safe-space sign in his office and does not particularly care to have them in his writing center. This berainbowed signifier of welcome, of a space inclusive and, ultimately, "safe" for queer people, does not speak to him. If he has to display a sign, he tells me, he has not done adequate work in crafting and honing his site. John names labor in his refusal to display a sign. He forgoes what he considers, perhaps, to be a sign of inactive "slacktivism" and the criticisms that might ensue while also pushing himself and his staff to do the work that creates an inclusive site. Claiming discomfort with ever being described as a "gay writing center director"—an identifier he feels isn't complimentary—he hopes to model, by example and by on-campus visibility, what a gay leader can do and be for their tutors and students. John's take on his work is complex.

On one hand, he exhibits discomfort with particular identifiers, such as activist stickers and gay-oriented titles. Yet, even with gentle dismissal of such traditionally activists actions, he does indeed walk the walk and do the labor in line with ways other participants describe specific forms of administrative queer activism, especially in embodied visibility and queer world-making. John's disidentification with an inclusive display sign is a form of labor in that he must face and respond to a campus climate that might call out his controversial perspective, and he must also walk the walk to do the work that deems such a safe-space sign irrelevant in the first place. As we see in earlier and later sections, John is not the only gay male participant to express discomfort with a *gay* descriptor for his administration.

Other participants note identity orientations to activist labor in writing centers. For these writing center directors, the work of writing centers is often the work of an activist, whether self-imposed or called for by others or by institutions or even evoked. In this vein, Cara tells me she is "an out queer writing center director," explaining that "that is [her] identity." She goes on: "I think being a writing center director is about an orientation to writing. I think being a queer feminist woman, that's also about orientation to people, to research, to scholarship." Cara discusses two complementary orientations—her intersectional queer feminist identity and her writing center administration. For Cara, her orientations are always in conversation. In this sense, current writing center research and its local and global disciplinary impact that grounds this chapter mirror Cara's orientations to her work. When juxtaposed with recent calls for radical writing center praxis, especially related to Greenfield's (2019) call for a new paradigm grounded in a new language and orientation to writing center work, Cara is perhaps the quintessential queer activist practitioner. She demonstrates and identifies with a writing center administrative identity that mirrors the field's definitions and calls for such work. Arguably, such activity is, by definition, still work and on a sliding scale between visible and invisible labor.

Such work does not end with herself, as Cara encourages her tutors to think strategically about how they do their work. She notes her queer orientation often leads her to encourage her tutors to call out writers in the current political landscape. Her queerness, she says, makes it possible, if not critical, that she "speak up" with regularity. She says,

> Consultants often want to fall back on, "Well, does this awful thing you said in your paper support your argument? Is there logic behind it?" And kind of approaching from this kind of logic, writerly standpoint instead of

calling people on their shit, and I'm all about, "Well, as a feminist queer woman, I just want to call you on your shit."

She pauses to say that such calling out can happen politely and adds, "I'm not advocating that we attack our clients, but I am advocating for speaking up. It's not about, 'Well did you say, have you considered all of your audiences,' no, saying, 'This is offensive' and 'This is wrong' and just really speaking up and being an ally." Cara's work of "speaking up" extends from her writing center to her National Writing Project (NWP) site, where she says her center's mission and her own queer administrative perspectives inform her NWP.

She tells me,

> When I had some [elementary-school] teachers who were like, "I don't think we can talk about [race and sexuality] with students. I don't think they're ready," I thought, "What the [f——] are you talking about?" I'm like, "That is a complete position of privilege to say that we don't need to talk about this. You're talking about fifth graders." I said, "If you have a single child of color in your classroom, they've already been talking about this their whole lives. If in your classroom you have two moms or two dads, they've already been talking about this their whole lives." I said, "My daughter is three years old. She's biracial with two moms. She has been dealing with these issues her whole life, and so for you to not talk about them actually sends her a very particular message."

Cara says she did not necessarily call out the NWP teacher, but she did use a "call in" technique (Tran 2013), where she privately and compassionately discussed the matters with the teacher (a technique sometimes controversially counter to "calling out" someone). She uses her center's mission and her own administrative practices to draw attention to activist orientations to identity and writing critical to higher education and all levels of the education field. Such an instance is why I struggle to name such moments as advocacy over activism. On one hand, Cara uses her identity, her administration, and her position of authority to work with, alongside, and perhaps subversively when calling out and calling in. However, while Cara is inside "the system" and works within a neoliberal institution (i.e., higher education), her work is directive in that she explicitly addresses methods for confronting an NWP participant's perhaps narrow understandings of elementary-education pedagogy. Cara's activist work exhibits directiveness paired with subversion.

Speaking up, as Cara does, suggests that her articulated identity—an out lesbian writing center director—is bound up in and informed by her work itself, similar to Tim, though distinct from his in how each names their work identity. Tim's discomfort with calling himself "the gay writing

center director" or with directing a "gay writing center" run counter to
Cara's administrative orientations. Similarly, Tim reflects both on his
former tutor and current director identities, noting a naïvete in practitioners who say writing center directorships—and, by extension, writing
centers—are neutral sites. In the opening vignettes, he notes using his
site to do activist queer work his institution hadn't done, such as holding
an AIDS Day event (i.e., the event that spawned perpetual condom and
sexual-health-resources access in his center). He says,

> The Writing Center's not Switzerland. There is no place that you can
> go as a tutor, no place that the writing center can be positioned that
> doesn't have some impact, even if it's just the impact of silent complicity.
> I've always been pushing the other way. To what extent can we embrace
> activists, pedagogies? Our logo, or our slogan for our writing center is,
> "Engaged on paper, engaged in life."

In his writing center theory and composition courses, he tells me, he
rarely "lays low" when bringing queer and justice and activist topics into
these curricula, especially his tutor training course. He tells me, "That's
where the energy is. It's also where the landmines are, but you have to
negotiate that stuff, it doesn't go away just because you ignore it." Tim
does not adopt the identifiers Cara does, but his labor is no less extensive
in such regard, especially his mention of heading into landmines to do
the work of writing centers in tutor training. This project regularly signaled participants to tell me that they didn't do writing center activism
but, normally alongside later descriptions, their labor seemed to reflect
activist orientations and that far exceeded the field's parameters for writing center work. The pause to tell me he is not "the gay writing center
director" while also telling me the "writing center's not Switzerland" may
speak to a disciplinary discomfort with what gay writing center directors
do in the discipline and even how Tim's discomfort might help me make
a claim that it is not just gay and queer people who do and ought to do
this work. Tim's discomfort may suggest that a writing center director,
regardless of identification and orientation, ought to adopt these particular ideals (i.e., the writing center as a political site that's certainly
not Switzerland) regardless of identifications, which is to say that Tim's
identification and direct administrative action may speak most to nonqueer audiences in that, unlike Cara, he does not think of his identity in
relation to his activist work, however married the two may seem.

Such disparities arise with other participants. After discussing what
he would tell young queer Black men about safe sex and the avoidance
of barebacking, James also tells me his writing center "isn't taking over.
I don't represent it as the writing center's doing this. It's just I'm doing

this and I happen to be the writing center coordinator. My tutors focus on praxis. On helping students with their papers." Here, he designates a boundary between activist work and writing center work, despite making distinct claims about how he may ultimately save and bring awareness to Black queer lives.

Saving lives is also in the purview of Jack, a transgender participant, who believes just living his life may impact his tutors, writing center, and institution.

> Maybe their kid in fifteen years comes out as trans, and they're not happy about it, and they wish it weren't the case. But maybe they'll remember me and think, "Maybe I don't have to be scared that my kid is going to be unhappy and be beaten up or whatever." I'm not a director who gets up on the pulpit. I will if somebody asks me to. But mostly it's so just, if you're in somebody's life, make sure you're doing whatever it is so that when they wake up tomorrow morning, the first thing they think of isn't, "I don't know why I should get up."

Queer administrative work identities are about a means to call out and be visible. Some expressively articulate a queer writing center administrative identity, as Cara does, but some also believe that identity can save lives, as Jack and James, do—a transgender and a Black participant. Yet, the occasional backtrack exists, an insistence that the work is just the conventional work of the writing center, work that happens to be led by a queer practitioner with particular queer values. Jack, for example, does not administer his site from a "pulpit," he says, nor do James or Tim seek to be the queer directors. Nor do the directors want a writing center that "takes over" or that is overly activist or "gay" in its orientation, to use Tim's identifiers (i.e., "the gay writing center director," "the gay writing center"). There is a regular distinction between the queer director who does particular queer-focused labor and those who do such work but do not name it as such nor think of it as central to their writing center mission. These discussions of work present a tricky dynamic. While nearly all participants in the project identify with activism, these four administrators note a relationship between a queer orientation and administrative identity; some, however, do the work but do not seek to name it in particular ways beyond conventional writing center administration purviews. An out lesbian woman with a background in queer theory and women's studies, Cara, "an out queer writing center practitioner," does not disassociate her writing center work from her personal, professional, and academic identities. Cara is certainly the administrator who models justice-focused orientations in her work. While perhaps less forthcoming about his writing center administration, Tim exposes discomfort with an identity and identifier, perhaps because of onsite tensions he mentions in chapter 4 when he reflects upon administrative stresses, disclosing fears of being perceived as lecherous in regard to male tutors and students. With this in mind, a danger could exist for Tim should he think of or name himself as a "gay writing center director" in the way Cara does—much of his work is distinct and often invisible but has potentially visible ramifications.

Jack, James, and Care are focused on their work's long-term impact. I argue that queer people gravitate to fields that afford opportunities for helping others—social work, medicine, education. It is likely no accident that queer writing center directors with activist professional orientations find themselves doing the kind of work described in this chapter. Of the twenty project participants, each does their own work, which certainly reflects activism. Cara names her work identity alongside queer identifiers and orientations, while others do similar work and avoid such identifiers. It is notable that this project's men are more likely to be bullied for their out, administrative orientations, as we see in later chapters. Such a reality suggests it may be difficult for Jack and James to be out and proud. Cara, indeed, does have a secure writing center directorship at a research-intensive, midwestern university that takes seriously and values her queer writing work and administration. Tim is tenured at his midwestern site, but his history of coming out "late," as he calls it, and feeling relatively reserved in his outness could speak to his discomfort about being the "gay writing center director," alongside Jack's and James's stances of staying away from identificatory "pulpits" but still doing work that is textbook activism. Denny (2011) teaches us that writing centers themselves—especially the work of one-to-one tutoring—have subversive potential in higher education. The disidentificatory naming practices of Tim, Jack, and James certainly gesture toward subversion, in that they do not call attention to their identities in the way Cara does, but their writing center work is no less life-saving. While several participants outrightly name and identify themselves as queer or gay writing center directors who orient to their administrations actively, the writing center work of, say, lower-key transgender education or safe-sex education for queer, Black men is not historically disparate from how queer communities' most disenfranchised have always had to operate. Naming a practice or an identity—being explicitly out—has always had repercussions. When queer people must help and save each other, we often must do so under the radar. Queer movements have rightly begun to suggest that being "out and proud" is never without risk. The lives of people who are out are still in danger in some Western and global cultures (see this book's literature review and its tensions chapter). As readers, I want to direct us away from the twenty-first-century idea that out and proud is always "activism" and keeping a tight lip is always "closeting." Practices and identities that are unnamed often have much subversive potential to make change and impact and save lives. Tim, Jack, and James may afford the writing center world just as much as Cara does in her out-and-proud administrative identity.

To remove unintended and potential rose-colored interpretations of this conversation, it's important to note this labor of activist work falls on, and is self-imposed by, queer people. In pointing out where this labor falls, I do not mean to imply a naiveté about these participants' perspectives. I believe in the labor of activist writing center administration and believe my queer orientation affords a nuanced lens for doing such work. But I merely hope to continue shedding light on the fact that much of this work falls on, and is self-imposed by, minority administrators, namely the field's queerest and, often, most vulnerable—a framework that will close this chapter.

QUEER ADMINISTRATIVE IDENTITIES AND POSITION TYPES

Along these lines, it would be irresponsible for me not to circle back to this chapter's early conversation about position type and queer writing center identity and approach, which aligns with a 2018 IWCA presentation that brought sobering but necessary light to the 2018 conference theme focused on social justice. There, Marilee Brooks-Gillies, Nicole Emmelhainz, Deirdre Garriott, and Scott Whiddon (2018) spoke about doing social justice pretenure without secure administrative positions in writing centers, showcasing a certain danger to such work from precarious position types. A necessary contribution to writing centers, the discussion did not quite align with participant perspectives of this book. Participants held diverse university positions across a host of institution types and regions. In only one case was discussing labor conditions made difficult based on the participant's university standing (i.e., at the time of the study, she was in an at-will, full-time staff position). Academic lore might suggest East Coast participants would be most secure (in position), most out, most activist, and most fearless when discussing their writing center labor; this was rarely the case in this study. Many of this project's most politically active did not hold tenure-line positions; they held staff writing center positions alongside nontenure-track faculty, instructional faculty positions, and adjunct faculty roles, while one participant, who was quite forthright about his orientations to his work, hailed from a high-school writing center. Many participants who discussed activist labor most vehemently worked in southern or southeastern states, or at conservative institutions with religious missions. Many participants who spoke about being out activist queer people at their sites were also pretenure, like Jeremy and Casey, neither of whom were fazed by approaching their sites with such orientations, despite Casey's direct report asking her to make room for more diverse perspectives on one occasion (we see these perspectives in the next section). In fact, only a few participants directly mentioned that tenured positions offered them particular positive affordances (Madeline and Tim), while Mike mentions in the next chapter that he experienced as much homophobia pretenure as posttenure. Cara, at the time of this study, was not in a tenure-line position but did hold an esteemed faculty and administrative position linked to a generous budget and strong relationships with upper administration who understood and respected her administrative vision.

This study's participants in at-will or staff positions happened to have supportive direct supervisors or upper administrations. However, I do not suggest such landscapes are typical for queer directors as a whole. There is a danger to concluding that, because most of these participants—most of whom are white and cisgender—have ideal labor landscapes, the writing center field should conclude our field's labor conditions are always already safe for all its laborers. Such a mentality—and even our field's recent scholarship, even those pieces that encourage bravery over safety—may still negatively impact our queer administrators, despite white, privileged, national sentiments that suggest queer people no longer experience oppression and writing center scholarship that suggests collective resolution for all stakeholders. For at least two participants in this study (and countless others in the field), being brave at their sites may connote danger: one, Jennifer, told me that, despite her supervisor's awkward mention that she (Jennifer) couldn't be fired for her sexuality even if that was administration's desire, the possibility of termination for her outness crossed her mind often.

An instance of labor that might best illustrate this tension in this kind of work and the participants' position types lies in Casey's work. Her institution's (a women's college) transgender policy spawned a writing center 'zine project, which was initiated, in part, by a few of her transgender tutors. The 'zines took off in the center and the campus community but spurred criticism from upper administration, who told Casey the 'zines weren't academic texts and advised that writing center projects should not delve only into transgender issues but also should address other topics. Casey took such news well but joked that she eventually took up the "fine, everyone's doing a 'zine" approach to writing center projects, encouraging all writing center consultants to build activist projects from social justice orientations and interests. Pretenure, Casey did not back off from work critical to her tutors, to her students, and, ultimately, to the world at large. Because she identifies as a queer pansexual person herself—an identity oft removed from queer communities and conversations, similar to bisexuality in its erasure—Casey's work is pressing, and she knows it. Like so many other participants, she must act, tenured or not.

RESPONDING TO NATIONAL EVENTS

Women's and LGBTQA Marches

A participant in the women's marches following the 2016 election of Donald J. Trump, Katherine discloses she "never imagined that [she] would be an activist and go to a rally to support women's causes, and LGBTQ, and all of these things out in the public. Even ten years ago that would have been unimaginable to [her]." The writing center, she says, has helped "further [her] advocacy for LGBTQ people and issues." She explains,

> I think if I had ended up in a comp job, I would still be struggling with issues of who to come out to and when to come out, but because I came to this spot I made the decision from day-one that I was going to be completely out. I knew I could do that and I knew that this place would support me in that. So, now I think I could go to any job anywhere and be completely out and open and either they accept it or they don't, but that's not on me.

Katherine is exmilitary. Clinton-era Don't Ask Don't Tell policies kept her closeted for many years, she tells me. It was her director and this writing center that encouraged her to be more out and open.

Her work orientations likely relate to her writing center site itself. As a then-associate director at a major research site, collaborating with a director with a social justice mission, Katherine worked in what the field might consider a writing center materially and metaphorically representative of an ideal site for radical writing center work (Greenfield 2019). As an example of the site's capacities, the center's tutor-training course is grounded in social justice writing center research, and as part of the course's final project, new tutors paint a ceiling tile with something that best represents them and helps them transition onto the writing center staff (i.e., many ceiling tiles include queer and activist signifiers, such as rainbow flags and transgender insignia). Its director,

Cara, tells me that the center's mission inevitably draws queer under-graduate and graduate tutors, relaying that writing centers are queer sites themselves by definition and default—spaces located in institutions of higher education but not quite classrooms, not quite sites of pedagogy, and not quite instructionally based with clear demarcations of power between "teacher" and "student." Katherine and Cara's space and mission make responding to national events part of their site's landscape, which is to say Katherine's marching in response to a national event is within the parameters of this kind of writing center work. Such a site makes possible movement in the direction of doing traditionally activist labor.

Marching at an activist event and being a writing center director may "empower and encourage" tutors, she says, pausing to tell me she regu-larly saw tutors at those events. Katherine believes in the near fusion of queer leadership and embodied visibility, especially the importance of a queer person at the helm of a writing center. In this sense, Katherine's event-based participation aligns with recent claims that writing centers are always already radical sites for combatting various oppressions (Greenfield 2019). She does queer activist labor in that such an orienta-tion is not a mere afterthought but a tangible representation of writing center administrative work. Katherine's mention of the relationship between her administration and her queer identity marks a theme that arises often in this chapter and that aligns with broader activist orientations that date back decades, especially related to visibility. Her rhetorical decision to discuss this visibility is specifically linked to a set of national events—a series of movements that speak to 2016's women's and LGBTQA rights. Like John, whom we hear from next, Katherine focuses on her visibility, yet a question, for me, arises: how visible is her work to her institution and within the parameters of her job duties? Katherine and other project participants teach us about nuanced queer writing center work that is gratifying and that also may come at a cost, as this chapter discusses in its conclusion.

2016's Orlando's Pulse and 2010's Case of Tyler Clementi

John was directing a writing center near Orlando when the 2016 *Pulse* Night Club tragedies took place—the events that opened this book. Noting that the local university had difficulty responding outside of policy and protocol, he says,

> It was so terrible to be here in Orlando at that moment, so horrifying. Being in the writing center was just really a gift, but very, very quickly, students wanted to talk. We came up with the idea of just having an

afternoon where we would invite anyone to come and write and share their writing. Whatever they got and whatever they wrote was fair game and it was so emotional and hard, but the writing center became a place where people could talk about the stuff they weren't talking about elsewhere.

While the event was not without its tensions and was traumatic for students and tutors, especially since a few tutors on his staff knew *Pulse* victims—a conversation forthcoming in another chapter—John tells me that the event was transformational for the community, but he struggled with his feelings. A white upper-middle-class gay man, he worried such an event "wasn't [his] tragedy" to mourn. He felt any mourning or particular kinds of writing center leadership related to the events might not be appropriate for him, given his status, race, and class, since the victims were mostly queer and transgender people of color from working-class backgrounds—none of which are identifications he holds, minus his queer one.

Whether the event was his tragedy to mourn or not, his tutors stepped in, asking for his leadership and support—labor necessary that his privilege did not make less emotionally and spiritually trying. I understand these requests. In a book chapter about responding to national events through digital and online writing, I chronicled my experience with the *Pulse* tragedies as a queer writing center director myself. As I mentioned in this book's opening as well, I feared much—saying or doing the wrong thing, being overly political in my writing center, and not being the right person to address the *Pulse* murders. Yet, one by one, my tutors dropped by my office, shut the door, and encouraged me to say something. They needed me to act. I wrote them to them, and I recounted these events in my published research. The email I wrote said,

> Hi, all,
>
> I've not said much about the Orlando events publicly, but I certainly feel their weight and am attuned to the fact that violent events such as these have deep impact on our academic communities. Moments like this can make us feel confused, helpless—even hopeless. As writing studies practitioners, though, we play an important role. As a local and global "face" and "voice" of writing, we have the power to help shape, and when necessary, support the revision of writing, rhetorical structures, and cultural arguments that position particular groups in problematic, if not oppressive, ways. A gunman who opens fire on LGBTQ people (mostly working-class and of color) in a public safe-space does so, at least in part, because western culture offers countless arguments and compositions in favor of metaphorical and material violence—through anti-LGBTQ legislation,

through groups and leaders who spout and write hatefully, through spoken and written micro-aggressions aimed at marginalized groups. With Harry [Denny] last April, we started a particular conversation, and I encourage us to move forward with a similar line of thinking—with attention to how a multi-pronged focus on consulting, identity, intersectionality, and inclusivity can positively impact our local and global communities. Our support of the LGBTQ writer who comes out to us through an expressive writing prompt matters. Our acknowledgement and use of the preferred pronouns of a transgender-identifying client matters. Our gentle challenge to a student's potentially racist argumentative essay matters. Each example is an actual instance (of many) where our center has supported an inclusive, intersectional vision for writing support. Let's keep moving forward—keep doing our part as writing studies practitioners.

No matter how deep I get into university administration, part of me will always be a LGBTQ Studies and Queer Rhetorics professor and academic activist committed to helping people make sense of challenging, if not difficult, topics. If you need anything in regard to the recent Orlando events, please don't hesitate to drop by. Happy to talk, to listen, to offer readings and resources—whatever you need.

In solidarity,
Travis (Hallman Martini and Webster 2017a, 282–83)

Like John, I wasn't sure if this event was my tragedy, but my staff called me to act. This calling is often both gratifying but is also rife with invisible labor—a theme of this book. It is invisible in process, but it is not a seamless product, as certainly this email was a tangible representation of labor but difficult to frame as conventional, "countable" writing center work. Yet, I wouldn't have acted any other way, as John and other participants say of intensive writing center work in a queer body.

Similarly, Adam tells me that the 2010 death of Tyler Clementi—an East Coast college student publicly outed via his roommate's digital distribution of Clementi's sexual encounter, which caused Clementi to commit suicide (Rose 2010)—was transformational for him (Adam) in his thinking about why he wanted to pursue writing center leadership. The writing center world had taken up this event in some capacity on the WCenter listserv through Denny's (2010), Sloan's (2010), and others' prodding leadership to challenge writing center colleagues to understand the impact of Clementi's passing on writing center sites. That is to say, these 2010 listserv messages certainly called out the writing center world for its silence on the matter, which has historically been a critique of the writing center discipline for its orientation to merely the practice of writing center tutoring (Hallman Martini and

Webster 2017b). Adam tells me that he, like Tyler Clementi, "[came] from the margins" and saw a direct link between this event and his own writing center leadership. A self-described "mother hen" to his tutors, Adam creates space for safety and bravery—two theoretical terms of current writing center research and practice (Hallman Martini and Webster 2017b; Rose 2016). He links this space-making to formal writing center classes and weekly staff meetings he and his tutors develop together. His own sexual orientation and gender performance allow him, he says, to live more comfortably and vulnerably—two approaches he sees as informing his understanding of writing and writers and that he says make him more attuned to understanding vulnerability, marginality, and privilege. He says the Clementi events and his own acceptance of himself as a queer person inform his consciousness that he is "at the helm of the writing center."

Six years apart, these events—the Pulse shooting and the Tyler Clementi suicide—speak to moments of queer violence, atrocity, and fatality. Despite a Western culture and even global signifiers related to queer equality and equity—especially queer marriage access across nations—violent atrocities with the goal of queer harm and death prevail and pervade. Transgender women of color are murdered at rates that have remained steady for decades. Prior to June 2020, with the passing of queer- and trans-friendly Supreme Court rulings in most states, queer people could be fired from their jobs and evicted from their homes for being out. When he was in office, President Trump perpetuated rhetorical and material harm to queer and transgender communities with half-witted, homophobic, and transphobic Tweets that, at best, positioned queer and transgender rights as up for debate, including a transgender military ban (Trump 2017), and, at worst, crafted a culture of queer fear that continues to elicit violence. Denny (2011) and Denny et al. (2019) instruct us to understand that the world at large embeds itself in writing center work. To take such claims a step further, this work—these queer responses to national events—speaks to laborious necessity described above in that queer identities are embedded in these events. These two queer practitioners, John and Adam, do not and, perhaps cannot, merely ignore these events: the events are at the forefront of their experience. Even when they might seek to keep to themselves about such atrocities, others, often from well-intentioned positionalities, expect queer people to act in such ways by speaking and acting out. When I was a writing center director, my staff expected as much of me, and I am not alone in experiencing such an expectation, as this chapter suggests.

These rhetorical administrative actions are never without tutor audiences, nor without labor. Responding to national events that impact queer people is arguably not on the administrative radar of all practitioners. One only needs to look at the years it's taken for our major writing center organizations to move beyond disciplinary orthodoxies of dated debates (Denny, Nordlof, and Salem 2018) to understand such a claim. Doing the full repertoire of writing center labor conventionally understood and outlined earlier in this book (Grutsch McKinney 2013) alongside a queer-centered inclination is work, it's labor, and it's quite rewarding labor but certainly no less trying, no less queerly laborious for its rewards. In this book's tensions chapter, Mike highlights his perceptions of a day in the life of straight white male writing center director at research-intensive sites. In his reflections, he notes these men appear to be without much stress and able to write prolifically, with lighter engagements on their identity. That is, they are not responding to national events that evoke their identities; their tutors are not encouraging them to write comforting emails in the face of identity-based atrocities, which is not to critique these kinds of straight white male administrators but to note their labor may be different from that of this project's queer practitioners.

National Events, Mental Health, and Transparent Vulnerability

In the age of posttruth rhetorics (McComiskey 2017), in which logic and rationality take a backseat to bullshit, irrationality, and feelings, both Dana and Ryan note that their own fears about the current landscapes, often for queer people and for Western culture in general, drive many conversations, if not work, with tutors, queer and nonqueer alike. As a writing center director, Ryan notes that life under the Obama administration was jarringly different from life under the Trump administration, expressing that once-valued things like reason and science are now more aligned with strongly held beliefs than with rationality and evidence. Dana tells me, "I think transparency and mentorship is so urgently needed right now. Tutors need to hear, and see, and be validated like when I feel scared about political things, and to see how I work through that because, I am scared about political things." With this said, both note their administrative transparent vulnerability often helps mediate such fears; they rely on "critical thinking and knowledge mitigating" or just being human and recognizing their abilities and their limitations when supporting tutors through the same grim global realities they face themselves. Like Dana, a vulnerable, transparent writing center administration, in which Casey's own mental health is intentionally talked about, is part of her queer leadership.

Dana says that, in this regard, she finds herself "performing being human" by articulating her own fears about political and cultural landscapes to tutors with regularity. Dana is one participant who regularly supports the mental health of tutors in general but also as it relates to their fears about such landscapes. To her staff, she is out about her mental health, regularly talking to them about her panic and anxiety, some of which was linked to being a queer person during the Trump administration—an institutional and cultural moment that instilled fear in many people with diverse intersectional identities. Driven by removing shame and fear from discussions of mental health, Casey "came out to tutors as having anxiety and depression, and that was the first coming out moment," which has offered them vehicles for doing the same. Such labor is gratifying but also occasionally makes it necessary for her to be off campus so she can fulfill her tenure-track commitments to research. Articulated transparency about fear, then, is not merely helping tutors navigate their own mental health but is also offering a queer administrative space, where she has helped tutors navigate an array of mental-health issues, including suicidal ideation resulting from queer oppression.

Similarly, Dana has come out in such ways to tutors in order to help them grapple with various instances linked to their conservative region and even to their lived experiences with suicidal ideation and queer violence. Such coming out and unconventional writing center support go hand in hand with this chapter's sexual-health discussion in that writing centers may be sites for such activism when queer people are at the helm. It would be difficult to engage with discussions of queerness and queer sexuality without including the mental health of queer people in that queer people are historically targets for oppression and violence, given the heteronormative Western landscapes. To add insult to injury, medical communities have historically pathologized such mental illness in queer people without contextualizing how Western and global cultures position queer bodies. Green (2018), speaking as a person of color whose emotional labor is vast and encompassing, especially as it relates to the work of Black Lives Matter, identifies such work as "exhausting. Those fighting on the front lines struggle with emotional turmoil and anguish. I know one too many people of color in higher ed who have PTSD and depression disorders from fighting this war at 'home'" (19). Such local and global phenomena that exert these burdens on people of intersectional difference are not separate from the work of writing centers (Denny 2011; Denny et al. 2019). In fact, this book's participants regularly note exhaustion similar to Green's—an exhaustion that stems from labor not formally or explicitly acknowledged in our work, such as that articulated in this chapter and throughout this book. In this sense, these queer practitioners often additionally volunteer their compassionate administration to take care of their queer and nonqueer tutors' mental health. Yet again, we have queer writing center practitioners quite literally saving lives, as mentioned in the previous section, which brings the writing center world into such topics as barebacking, PrEP, condoms, and dental dams. This time, they are supporting mental and emotional health in addition to sexual health.

The current political landscapes for queer people bring forth exigencies. Dana notes an urgency for which her queerness may offer tutors means for engaging with the world through writing center work: "We have weekly staff meetings to increase all of the students' capacity for understanding that diversity is a lot more than like, 'Be nice to black people.'" She notes that such work is directly about her queerness in the writing center but also intersects with race and antiracism. She says, "I feel greater urgency than ever before to do more than be passively progressive, like in the difference between not being racist and being antiracist. Modeling how we can have productive conversations about fear feels really important right now." It is this urgency driven by concern and fear—this administrative vulnerability—that informs Dana's queer administration. Conversely, Madeline tells me, "I am not afraid of anything." She extends her claim:

> That's probably because I'm in a very privileged position, so I can voice things. If I hear things, I can voice my reaction. So I can imagine times when a conversation was going in a direction that wasn't going to be useful for anybody, and I would step in and say, okay, we need to think about the fact that you're leaving out people who might be gay or transgender. So I don't have any problem doing that, but I also don't feel like I'm a person who's representing a whole group of people, although I can tell you, I've been put in that position a couple of times [as a writing center director].

In another chapter, Madeline even notes her ability to "roll right over" tensions, a thread examined in this book's tensions chapter, offering a perspective counter to other participants'. Yet, her lack of fear does not give way to apathy. She speaks about and does activist labor in ways reflective of this chapter's other participants, as showcased in later book chapters.

I end this chapter's participant perspectives on a note of vulnerability. This decision aligns, partially, with the next chapter, which examines how participants interface with tensions often ignored or written off as irrelevant to current political landscapes, especially by straight administrator counterparts. Queer labor-related fear is often beyond the parameters that a writing center administrator may feel on a given day at their site. Certainly, we all may fear losing our jobs, whether we hold tenure-stream, full-time permanent staff, liminal, or part-time contingent positions. As writing centers close or are reassigned to other units, or as universities themselves close, professionals in all areas feel tensions that impact our job security and our feelings about our work. As higher education continues to face a prospectively crumbling landscape, fear makes its way into our daily lives, a reality true for any stakeholder perhaps. With this said, simply being, simply existing in a space, any space, may impact the orientation to fear for these queer writing center professionals, which ultimately does not merely impact their work but in actuality is labor, as we see here with Dana and Ryan and in the next chapter. The manner in and frequency with which fear arises is perhaps often ignored when we think about what it means to be a queer writing center laborer in the current political landscape. What is additionally left out of our administrative conversations is the way queer and nonqueer tutors alike look to queer writing center professionals to assuage fears, whether related to mental health or to being queer in Western culture, which is at once progressive, regressive, and oppressive.

CONCLUSION

Participants name, experience, and do their activist work in ways we have not yet encountered in published writing center research. Claims about the writing center acting as a de facto site for sexual-health advocacy and HIV prevention, for example, have not surfaced in our field's leading journals or book-length studies. Futher, little writing center research delves into mental-health concerns of administrators and tutors, outside of writing center scholarship that attends to mental illness in discussions of disability in relation to visiting students or tutors (Degner, Wojciehowski, and Giroux 2015). For fear of superficially representing this book's participants, I am hesitant to claim that queer writing center directors are always special unicorns, as I did in chapter 2, that wield and yield progressive, activist magic in their administration (this book suggests, however, that their histories and activisms are quite magical for making knowledge about administrative work in the writing center field). In the cases examined in this chapter, queer people are bringing to the table their lived experiences that they then apply to their work; they exhibit queer capital (in another chapter) related to their experiential readiness for their work. I do claim, though, that these practitioners labor distinctly and differently based on their queer orientations. Arguably, all directors labor with nuanced orientations to work that, in some capacity, reflect their identities, but this empirical glimpse offers nuance that has long been theorized about, namely that writing centers are sites where a spectrum of politics and identities collide, often quite beautifully, sometimes quite complexly. Every instance of queer world-making a participant names is a glimpse into the reality that such orientations to the work is, indeed, distinct work, with queer people performing much of this labor locally and disciplinarily.

I conclude this chapter with a few claims that may be controversial, but I hope you will join me in the discussion as an accomplice (Green 2018) in understanding how these queer administrators carry out and understand their activist work. The work of listening is critical to the political moment. Green (2018) calls us to "stop bein' [allies]; instead be accomplices," articulating that allyship is silent in its support while accompliceship happens through "[demonstration]" and "word and deed" (29). The first step of that kind of work is to listen carefully to the queer stories in this project. Asao Inoue, in his 2019 Conference on College Composition and Communication chair's address, asked White participants to listen and to even experience discomfort to facilitate coalition building with people of color in order for the rhetoric and composition discipline to move forward.

Such accompliceship through listening to build coalitions is quite rare, even from self-disclosed allies and accomplices. Since becoming a writing center tutor in 2002, and holding faculty and staff administrative posts since 2015, I have heard more times than I can remember that all our work in writing centers, and rhetoric and composition by extension, looks similar. On one hand, there is camaraderie in being part of the writing center community. Ultimately, doing writing center work is fabulous, and the activist slant of our work is gratifying. Certainly, in preparing ourselves as well as the next generation of writing center administrators for twenty-first-century work, we do have a foundation for understanding the work of writing centers (Grutsch McKinney 2013). Yet, for every vote of confidence for this project, I get alternating reactions from colleagues in this subdiscipline known for its kindness, compassion, empathy, and even its activist slant. When I talked about this project at the IWCA Queer SIG, no less, I received versions of eye rolls, alongside a few comments from straight, white folks ("What does any of this have to do with my writing center and my work?"). The well-intentioned comments from allies are, perhaps, equally dismissive (i.e., "oh, yes, I do that, too [inserts story that doesn't in any way call upon their visible or invisible identities in their administration]"). When thinking about the activist work queer people in writing centers, please do consider the following statements:

Queer writing center directors are differentially and unilaterally positioned to do the work of writing center administrative activism. Because of this position-ing, these directors often are expected to or exert self-pressure to perform this labor.

Queer people of varied intersections, especially those of privilege, face pressure to be active in local and global communities. Whether through social media, grassroots politics, or local or national elections, the personal as political pervades much of current queer political land-scapes, especially following the 2016 presidential election. As I wrote this chapter, South Bend Indiana Mayor Pete Buttigieg placed a presidential bid for the Democratic nomination and ran for president of the United States, being the first to represent among gay male voices in the run for the United States presidency. Yes, he was a white privileged male plucked out of relative obscurity for his white privilege, and he was not particularly supported by droves of queer communities. With this said, representation matters. Activism matters. His run was made possible, in part, by decades of queer people, often on the margins, working from their lived experiences to make systemic change. With this backdrop, the writing center field tells us we ought to value social justice and activ-ism, but what does that mean for queer people, for whom the personal and the political are acutely present.

Anyone can put condoms in writing centers, certainly. Yet, this chap-ter's queer orientations to such activist work align specifically with queer practitioners' unique queer experiences. I wager that few straight writ-ing center practitioners know what PrEP or dental dams are without googling them. I make this statement not to shame or to be exclusive but to point out the complexity of historic and current conversations about LGBTQA and queer sex and its practices and ideologies. The identities of queer writing center practitioners in higher education are "taxed" by their students, tutors, colleagues, and institutions. That is, the labor exerted and expected from such practitioners, by themselves or external forces, is differential, nuanced, unique, and imposed. This uniqueness is perhaps related to special queer unicorndom but also to lived experiences, queer orientations, and cultural, institutional, site-based, and disciplinary expectations. Such parameters make queer writing center administrators the go-to people for matters that involve and extend beyond the writing center. That's how we end up with seemingly "off-topic" matters in these writing centers (e.g., condoms, dental dams, sexual and mental health) that are anything but. These queer practitioners because of their evoked identities do not have the luxury of simply ignoring their identities or their identities' engagement with particular kinds of work. Further, others, especially our straight white male colleagues, aren't likely to take up the slack in this work. But in all fairness, they couldn't do so if they wanted, as much of the labor described requires a queer body and LGBTQA sentiment.

This work is not the same as that for administrators of color, but it rhymes.

This book alludes to how labor is distributed, perhaps unevenly, to bodies of difference for the support of tutors, students, colleagues, sites, and, ultimately the broader culture. In this project, I make suggestions for how the writing center discipline could account for such labor in its mission and vision and revisit that conversation extensively in the book's conclusion. Recent research, such as Riddick and Hooker's (2019) *Praxis: A Writing Center Journal* special issue "Race and the Writing Center," unravels a writing center world and history distinct from conventional writing center conversations, especially in a field that is very white and very privileged (Valles, Babcock, and Jackson. 2017). My project's queer writing center labor, especially because of its predominantly white participant set, is not Black writing center labor. Such a statement is complex because the project includes two queer participants of color, of course. With this said, there is complementarity in the ways people of intersectional difference from historically marginalized groups perform or are expected to perform emotional and invisible labor, as we see in this chapter. As mentioned above, the labor is not the same, but it rhymes.

Supporting tutors' and students' sexual health and mental health are often part of the work of queer writing center directorship.

It could not be a surprise that these queer administrators' work is rife with implication for mental and sexual health. To circle back to this chapter's earlier argument, these directors are doing in their jobs what queer people have done for decades—saving each other and others.

Some audiences will be uncomfortable with the sex discussions of this chapter, and that's okay. Talking about it may save lives. James Zebroski (2014), a gay rhetoric and composition scholar who survived the early AIDS crisis, often begins his queer histories courses with the following statement: "Everyone I had sex with in the early to mid-1980s is dead." He notes the weight of talking about sex in his classrooms and the magnitude of living through a particular historical moment. He says that initiating such conversations with students, speaking to and about particular histories and practices, may, indeed, save students' lives. Talking about sex, sexuality, and sexual practices through literary and rhetorical studies may help students navigate those same frameworks in life outside academia. The same may be true of the labor of the practitioners in this study; the work, whether housing condoms, providing dental dams, or talking a mentally struggling queer tutor through a trying situation, may save the lives of another person, queer or not. These available condoms and dental dams aren't just political artifacts but a means for queer people to support others. We as queer people often do not have the luxury of shedding these identities and histories that comprise ourselves and our cultures as they relate to our work. Further, not all the people saved by this work are mirror images of these practitioners: this queer labor has implications beyond queer people, which is to say that these workers are not only focused on other queer people, whether students, tutors, or colleagues; they are focused on people—which may help nonqueer audiences relate to such work and such claims.

Queer writing center practitioners doing activist work aren't all in high-powered directorships at research-intensive institutions, nor are their universities necessarily in supposedly liberal areas of the country.

Conventional academic narratives suggest we can do the work or research we want to after tenure. While less conventional, similar logic implies that academic freedom and activist orientations to academic labor are unique to tenure-stream faculty. Yet, many of this chapter's most active participants do not hold faculty positions at all, instead filling full-time staff positions. While some are in established, protected positions at research-intensive institutions, many are pretenure. By extension, these writing center sites are not in New York City or San Francisco. No participant hails from either urban gay mecca, nor is any participant from the West Coast. These writing centers are in noncollege town midwestern states. They are in the urban and rural South. They are in small liberal arts colleges, sometimes private but often not. These realities challenge conventional wisdom about doing activism, where it can be done, and by whom. It is, perhaps, the complex interplay of queer people being drawn to and encouraged to look out for others and respond to community issues that makes this labor possible in so many seemingly unconventional sites, contexts, and bodies.

Queer writing center directors identify quite specifically with the work of the twenty-first-century writing center and its activist mission and vision, arguably because of the political moment for people of difference. Queer writing center administrators may revel in such activist orientations to writing center administration, but it is no less a form of distinct, nuanced labor that differs from non-queer colleagues' perspectives outlined in past and recent writing center and writing program administration literature, namely discussions of emotional labor. (Caswell, Grutsch McKinney, and Jackson 2016)

The political landscape in which queer people are both pedestaled and killed, depending on the event, makes it difficult for queer writing center practitioners to just sit in their offices and do only the conventionally named work of writing center administration. These queer practitioners' identities are regularly evoked nationally, locally, and disciplinarily. Some activist acts elicit choices (e.g., tutor training and writing center mission and vision) that any one practitioner might make, but the political backdrop makes particular kinds of labor impossible to avoid, such as engaging with tutors who identify us as someone who can help, when others can't take up the labor, especially our straight, white male colleagues. Often, queer practitioners are the only people who can do this labor. The activist work of this chapter is labor. It is often not compensated. It is sometimes accounted for in the review process, but often not. All participants name it positively, so much so that it's difficult to distinguish what they do as work from what they do as people of intersectional difference impacted by cultural landscapes. Writing centers as sites of activism and civic engagement pervade current disciplinary conversations—from peer-reviewed research to quotidian listserv conversations. Such conversations imply writing centers ought to uphold and sustain justice-focused orientations, in the first place, and that the writing center field's few diverse leaders ought to lead such activism on and off site. As this book's introduction argues, this work isn't necessarily emotional labor, or even always invisible labor, nor does it fit neatly into the parameters drawn for writing center work. Without collective awareness of and resources for such labor across institutions and disciplines, the writing center field's oft-articulated values may be unsustainable and unattainable and may rest potentially upon the field's most vulnerable, which is a specific closing tenet of this book.

Queer activism may impact research agendas and the discipline as a whole and be part of an "invisible CV," which is difficult to account for in university review processes, whether tenure stream or not.

Anne Ellen Geller and Harry Denny (2013) caution writing center practitioners about the work of writing centers, attending to how labor is accounted for in disciplinary research as well as job descriptions. Our institutions value research, and conducting and contributing research is the work of a scholar. Research often, indeed, may lead to better labor conditions for writing center practitioners, whether tenure stream or not. In such an arrangement, how labor is represented to institutions is a critical. What could be called an "invisible CV"—for example, helping a queer tutor find immediate resources for suicidal ideation—is difficult to present to an institution for review, whether or not the said queer practitioner is on the tenure track. Further, as a queer writing center colleague said to me recently, "All this writing center focus on activism is fantastic. But the field needs to figure out if it's activist or scholarly. And if it's both, it's needs to find better parameters and practices for articulating that connection." Ultimately, published research about queer and activist topics is relatively light, as this book's literature review suggests. The question becomes, what doesn't happen in the scholarship of the broader discipline, or in the scholarly trajectories of these queer scholars, when certain kinds of intensive queer labor do happen? Missing from the conversation is how this labor may be taken up and counted in order for these queer practitioners to better their labor conditions—that is, a glimpse into how the labor interfaces with institutions, with practitioner status (i.e, staff, pretenure, posttenure), with its translations (i.e., whether the work is research, administration, teaching, or service), with institution type, and with institutional region.

Disciplinary change surrounding activist writing center work is not needed or possible. It just needs to be understood differently and proactively supported.

I see no need to call for disciplinary change, nor for queer writing center directors to adapt their administrative approaches, to delegate this labor to others, or to balance it with other colleagues. I realize the controversy in such a statement, but these workers are uniquely equipped for this work. Who does and is asked to do this activist labor is complex, as is how tutors, students, peers, and administrators gravitate toward these administrators in the first place. Should labor among writing centers, departments, and collegiate units be distributed more evenly, with less burden upon queer people? Of course. Is it unlikely that queer administrators will suddenly abandon or shift their attention from these labors, and even further unlikely that straight white male writing center directors, for example, will take on these kinds of labors? Of course. In fact, the reality is that such changes to these labor dynamics would be awkward, if not useless, especially for those tutors, students, and fellow administrators for whom queer writing center administrative labor makes a critical difference. In this sense, the field must respond to such realities as they are in order to better support the holistic professional self and the development of queer writing center administrators.

In this sense, the discipline's flagship and regional organizations must make more space for intentional queer writing center mentorship across institution types and experience backgrounds. The IWCA has an LGBTQA Standing Group for practitioners to meet and discuss queer issues in their writing centers. At present, I colead the IWCA's SIG and recognize the value and history of its mission. But a meeting place is a meeting place; conversations, while fruitful, often don't leave the conference site and are often spaces for airing necessary grievances about home institutions. Space is made, but continued, tailored relationships are necessary, and perhaps naming folks' lived identities and experiences as "special interests"—instead of, say, standing groups—was a bit demeaning in the first place, given that the IWCA LGBTQA Standing Group was called a special interest group for many years. Further, while IWCA's Mentor Match Program does, indeed, account for queer identities when matching professionals, I do wonder how we as a profession may take up such initiatives more intentionally, across our sites and our affiliations. And perhaps our IWCA Summer Institutes could explicitly name and afford support for such labor. If we know the kind of labor queer practitioners may face—from studies such as this one—we must use this data to better prepare practitioners for labor such as that articulated by this project's participants. We must identify ways not to change the labor exerted on queer practitioners but to mitigate the work put upon these queer minority administrators.

While this chapter does not deal with participants' research (it will be covered in later chapters and the book's conclusion), we can infer that this nuanced work makes it difficult for the field's queer administrators to produce scholarship. Consequently, the IWCA and its affiliates must take the lead from their disciplinary affiliates that regularly fund and recognize queer projects and researchers through awards and recognitions, such as the Conference on College Composition and Communication's Scholars for the Dream Award, Stonewall Service Award, and Lavender Rhetorics Award. The IWCA Research Grant Committee did recognize a queer project in 2016 (this one). However, a continued focus on queer and diverse identity-focused projects could ensure better research capacities for queer practitioners, who may need additional resources to account for and propel scholarly production that could be stifled by their invisible and visible labor. In fact, Geller and Denny (2013), as noted above, remind writing center practitioners that "we become agents in our own marginalization if we are not disseminating scholarly knowledge through publication and are instead mired only in everyday intellectual labor" (120). Such attention to queer researchers may afford our field more diverse perspectives, especially through queer and raced research in writing centers, as mentioned by Brian, a participant of color, whom our field has not retained because of its lack of such research, among many reasons. To what extent our disciplinary organizations could support not just research but queer folks' advancement, per these distinct labors, is of utmost importance, whether in regard to tenure navigation, research support, or professional development.

PARTING WORDS TO TENSION

In May 2019, Nina West, a contestant on Season 11's *RuPaul's Drag Race*, was eliminated from the show following a poorly performed "lip-sync for your life," a practice standard of reality television trajectories, where the week's bottom-ranked queens competitively lip-synched to avoid elimination. Nina West was Season 11's most respected queen for her activism, philanthropy, and, ultimately, kindness, as she was often regarded for embodying positivity, sometimes an anomaly in drag and queer cultures. With the mantra "Go Big, Be Kind, Go West," West's departure was controversial, despite her eventually being given the coveted Season 11 "Miss Congeniality" award, as well as her service as a role model for the queer community of how a participant might use their celebrity status and reality television platform for activist purposes. West's philanthropy extends to queer and LGBTQA issues well beyond marriage equality and into transgender rights. Thus, her elimination was jarring for many, not just within the show's parameters but for what West has come to represent in queer, transgender, and drag communities.

Soon after the elimination, Congresswoman Alexandra Ocasio-Cortez chimed in to the conversation through videoed tweets and her Instagram Story. In those messages, Ocasio-Cortez said, "No spoilers, but to the queen that went home this week, just know how important you are to the bigger picture, and I'm so proud of you and your fundamental kindness and goodness." To many, her words of allyship, related to her naming West's commitment to the "big picture," were respected given that a straight, "woke" woman of color was drawing attention to an activist drag queen and gay man as a queer world-maker. Ocasio-Cortez named the realities of the current political moment—the labors, if you will—of the work of queer activism at a time when such activism is trying, distressing, and perhaps exhausting, but no less worth it, and not without its labors. This is an example of one laboring person understanding the critical labors of others. We need Nina Wests in the world for the queer work itself, and we need Alexandra Ocasio-Cortezs in the world to recognize, praise, and encourage the queer work and the queer labors. This account links back to this section's opening, with Green (2018) calling on us to understand and act for each other through "word and deed" (29). If you are reading this chapter as a straight person, I do not expect that you will understand every analytic morsel of this chapter, nor will you be able to identify with every experience-driven moment of labor. I only hope you will be an accomplice, even an ally; I don't mind alliance. But regardless, when you think about your writing center identity and about the labor of your queer colleagues, be Alexandria Ocasio-Cortez recognizing and encouraging Nina West. If you're not transgender, listen to Jack. If you're not queer, gay, or lesbian, listen to Tim and Cara, regardless. If you're not a queer person of color, listen to James (and Brian, of the previous and next chapters). See and listen to the big picture. Such minor but revolutionary action inevitably makes for better work environments and lived experiences for queer, transgender, and of color peers, given that writing center work and its parent universities can be ripe with tension for practitioners, as the next chapter discusses.

4

QUEER WRITING CENTER
LABOR AND/AS TENSION

HISTORICAL VIGNETTES

As a former AIDS organizer, Mike told people, "never trust trust." This advice refers to educating at-risk populations about not relying on trust—trust of sexual partners or trust of familiar situations—to stay HIV-negative during times of queer pandemic crises, such as the mid-1980s onslaught of queer deaths from AIDS infection. Mike tells me the phrase resonated with him at his previous university, where he was a tenure-stream and later tenured writing center director, an institution he ultimately left for another such position, where he is happier and has been bullied less. In retrospect, he reflects on early warnings signs that dated back to his campus visit; interviewers, who later became his colleagues, told him being out and gay was fine, but not "to sleep with [his] students"—advice that, to Mike, seemed oddly and specifically directed as his gay identity. Mike's trust for his work environment was a double-edged sword: on one hand, he built meaningful relationships with tutors, students, and many colleagues. On the other hand, his out sexuality was the subject of various explicitly homophobic epithets, not the least of which was a colleague calling him "the fag professor" behind his back to other professors, tutors, and students.

Jennifer told me that while she was a staff-level writing center administrator, she was afraid of coming out at work for fear of being fired. She came out to a client during a session, in a way that was relevant to the tutoring situation. She soon visited her supervisor's office to relay the situation and was met with support. The support was couched, however, in a comment that shook her. Her supervisor said, "Of course it's okay to be out here. I couldn't fire you if I wanted to." The supervisor likely intended the comment in good faith, Jennifer tells me. However, during the interview, both Jennifer and I paused and rustled with a bit of discomfort. Something about the word "couldn't" and the phrase "if I wanted to" didn't sit with either of us well.

Stephanie, a staff writing center director in the South, who identifies as lesbian and gender nonconforming, expresses general contentment with her

DOI: 10.7330/9781646421497.c004

position. Her tutors, many of whom are from conservative and religious backgrounds, regularly praise her leadership for giving them a diverse worldview. She and her colleagues are close as well, though she notices almost a cognitive dissonance in them because they often back conservative legislation and legislators who support anti-LGBTQA causes. In fact, she once overheard an otherwise trusted colleague note support for explicitly homophobic legislation. She wondered aloud to me how they could be work friends with her and not make the connection that such worldviews and such conservative voting could materially harm her queer body.

Jeremy, a writing center director in the North, went on a campus visit for a tenure-track writing center job he eventually took. His visit coincided with a 2016 Trump rally that exposed and gave voice to local homophobic and racist sentiments. An international student was, in fact, murdered around the time of Jeremy's visit as well. Unsurprisingly, authorities believed the two instances were linked. Not only did he feel direct tension between his queer body and the site itself, but he was deeply aware of how his writing center philosophy and queer-themed job talk might be subject to violence, harassment, or ridicule, if his on-campus presence was made public to the community

These stories convey that queer writing center directors face tensions distinct to their jobs and which comprise a significant part of their work. Such tensions, in fact, are work, as this chapter argues through its participant voices. Current writing center research tells us that the world itself plays out in our centers (Denny 2011; Denny et al. 2019; Greenfield 2019; Hallman Martini and Webster 2017b). Our labor, while perhaps not traditionally or explicitly headed with violence, does mirror the world writ large. Consequently, this chapter sheds light on the realities of how the world impacts localized, work-based tensions. Yet, in it, I hope to stay true to my word to a senior colleague who requested, tongue-in-cheek, that I not make this chapter "yet another" narrative piece in the field of writing centers and rhetoric and composition in which administrators complain about their jobs.

This chapter centers on tensions that surround participants' lived experiences. While it is not a chapter that focuses entirely on forms of bullying, the named tensions are a lava lamp of shifting instances and repercussions that invoke external bullying, mobbing, and aggressions, as well as disciplinary and national implications for such violence. Many participants—twelve of twenty in fact—named instances classified in recent rhetoric and composition scholarship as bullying. Using research in higher education, rhetoric and composition, and writing program

administration, Cristyn Elder and Bethany Davila (2019) define bullying as "incivility, mobbing, systemic bullying," extending the definition
from their examination of other higher education research to include
"harassment, social exclusion or isolation, rumors, criticism, and verbal
abuse," all of which take place regularly over time, while the scholars
remind us "minority status" in culture writ large often equates to the
same status in academia (6). For Elder and Davila (2019) bullying is
linked to a complex intermingling of power dynamics among bullies
and victims. Such power, however, is not easily pinpointed to simply
the bully outranking the bullied. Tenured faculty members, both in
broader academia and in this project, report bullying with regularity, as
this chapter examines. Further complicating this definition, the scholars
identify intention in that bullying entails "deliberate actions performed
by others that impede or disparage [our] work" (12) but that have
been historically clouded and hidden in euphemisms—"politics" and
"working conditions," for example (10–11)—which, the authors claim,
sidestep material conditions and ramifications for sites plagued by bullying cultures.

Other rhetoric and composition and writing center scholars name
narrative and theoretical frameworks for bullying. David Wallace (2002)
describes his process of being out in the academy and the various tensions and roadblocks he encounters as he navigates his institution as an
out gay man in the early 2000s. Denny (2014) explicitly describes bullying he experienced while a faculty writing center director and encourages us not to sweep such occurrences under the rug because they don't
fit a particular rubric of queer violence. In fact, he aptly claims that
we, in academia and in the writing center world, tend to overlook the
everyday nature of bullying, assuming real queer oppression happens to
other people; in situations in which we aren't complicit; and in grand
gestural violence like gay, queer, and trans "bashing" and murders (3–4,
6). Denny (2014) argues that we also don't recognize bullying when it
happens at first because academic administrative laborers are conditioned to "fumble and bumble to a new set of chops" (2) when starting
new positions and interfacing with unfamiliar institutions. Like Elder
and Davila (2019), he signals practitioners to challenge what has long
been simply blamed on departmental and institutional politics (2). Yet,
being bullied at work is violence and, as stated throughout the book, it is
work in its felt, emotional, and psychological impact and responses and
in its ramifications for the work of writing administration.

Elder and Davila (2019) note that the discipline often recites a
privilege-laden mantra that one ought not take up writing program

administration before tenure—an argument posited through disciplinary lore but also in contributions to Elder and Davila's collection (Matzke et al. 2019), especially those that call out the privilege in such disciplinary mantras. Many practitioners have little choice but to take on such professional responsibilities. Such circumstances as interim or acting assignments, pre- and posttenure service requirements, small institutions and departments, limited resources, interest in doing research, and even just the desire to do the labor all account for ways this post-tenure-only mantra remains impossible in rhetoric and composition and writing center administrative work. An avoidance mentality is not only impossible but is also, as is evident in this book's participant experiences, irrelevant, given the parameters of their job descriptions. Such sentiments do not surface often in the writing center world, with just 35–40 percent of writing center directors being tenured or tenure stream (Writing Center Research Project, n.d.) and with over half our discipline led by staff or administrative workers, most of whom do not have the luxury of waiting for or avoiding work for supposedly better labor conditions.

This chapter breaks tensions into four major sections: explicit and implicit bullying and disciplinary erasures and national tensions that impact participants' work, the latter of which are juxtaposed with the previous chapter's activism lens. I define bullying alongside the definitions of Elder and Davila (2019) and Denny (2014) and make the distinction between explicit and implicit to account for what James, a participant of color, calls tensions "you can't put your finger on," meaning they are hushed, perhaps whispered, but made apparent through under-the-surface passivities that enact violence upon queer bodies.[1]

Here, I reiterate the point that being bullied and responding to bullying and other work-based tensions are not merely offshoots of the work; they are work, work rarely talked about for its material implications upon and within writing center labor. And to echo the research-based sentiments of current rhetoric and composition scholarship, the avoidance of these material realities simply leads to reinforcement and normalization of the behaviors (Elder and Davila 2019, 12). Elder and Davila (2019) suggest rhetoric and composition and WPA scholarship of the past alludes to bullying but does not explicitly name labor as such, and I make the same claim about writing center research. Even the field's strongest and most current assessment of the state of writing center labor, such as *The Working Lives of New Writing Center Directors* (Caswell, Grutsch McKinney, and Jackson 2016), does not specifically name bullying as major factor in their participants' case studies, despite many instances that seem to represent bullying, especially the researchers' case studies of Allison, Anthony, Jennifer, and Katarina, in which upper-administrative forces and colleagues are roadblocks to new directors' work-based trajectories. In other words, like the rhetoric and composition and writing program administration fields, writing center administrative studies could benefit from further investigation into tensions such as these that interface with, complicate, and ultimately become our work.

TENSIONS: EXPLICIT BULLYING

"Never trust trust," Mike tells me, as he did in this chapter's introductory vignettes. To delve further into his story, during his stint as a midwestern 1980s AIDS organizer, this statement was his mantra. In those years, he used the words to encourage queer people to protect themselves from even the most trusted sexual situations and partners. He reflects on his previous writing center directorship. Such a statement, he says, is quite haunting: he used it to warn young queer men about safe sex in the early years of AIDS, but he says in actuality it speaks to his experience with bullying at his former institution. This doesn't feel like a stretch in the least. His voice shakes as he tells me the stories.

He trusted much about this institution: his colleagues, his tutors, and his center. But a series of pre- and posttenure events compromised that trust. In his first years in the profession, he was out and proud, framing his sexuality in his writing center administration, as many of this book's participants proudly and professionally do, where identity and administration often coalesce. During his second, pre-tenure writing center directorship, however, the "imprint of another director's administration" created a difficult scenario for him when he inherited it. The religious affiliation of the university was certainly a factor, which is to say the site had an occasional conservative slant, but Mike tells me this conservatism was merely "a pretext." It was "the easiest thing to latch onto as being problematic" as he navigated and ran up against "the ghosts of a prior administration." To add insult to injury, a staff person with whom he worked called him a "fag," while others, including colleagues, tutors, and students, rallied against him in various ways. He had many allies but no accomplices (Green 2018), in that few supported him in "word and deed" (29), merely expressing outrage at his situation. Alongside "fag" comments, he dealt with false accusations from and difficult power relationships with queer peers of varied ranks. He tells me he should have seen the red flags on his campus visit given that the search committee, upon his question about being out at a religiously affiliated institution, said, "Sure, just don't sleep with your students." He tells me they would never say that to a prospective straight candidate. I agree. He left the institution for a much better position where he isn't the object of homophobic slurs, among many other positive work-based realities, and he likens the former institution to an "abusive relationship."

I pause to acknowledge that Elder and Davila (2019) teach us that bullying is common. Mike's story is not anomalous. It is, perhaps, this quotidian nature that makes continued empirical and theoretical research about collegial relations in writing center administration necessary. Having participated for years in LGBTQA special interest meetings and standing groups for the International Writing Centers Association and the Conference on College Composition and Communication, I can say without hesitation that queer professionals and administrators in the writing center world and rhetoric and composition discipline regularly recount experiences that mirror Mike's perspectives and that corroborate Elder and Davila's (2019) exigence. Mike's stories, however, are especially haunting and grim. His story and others in this section show that such bullying is not implicit nor under the surface. It sits explicitly in day-to-day conversations between colleagues, with students privy. It includes a homophobic epithet (i.e., *fag*). It is embedded in this culture. A departmental environment in which a colleague calls another a "fag" speaks to a local culture that pervades and has already poisoned a community. My claim here is not to detract from either Mike's story nor the actions of his abusers but instead to cycle back to these instances as both unsurprisingly quotidian and eerily common. An abusive colleague has been empowered—by a department, by a superior, by perhaps an entire university culture. Higher education pats itself on the back often for its supposed progressive cultural missions. By extension, the writing center world tends to understand itself quite harmoniously from our "grand narratives," especially those that connote "comfort" for writing center stakeholders (Grutsch McKinney 2013). Stories like Mike's productively and systematically dismantle such naïveté.

Mike's experience may teach reader-administrators about a guardedness that pervades his and other queer men's writing center administration. Mike says he was an open queer mentor and director before these experiences. For a long while, however, he became quite guarded in all his relationships, even and especially with his queer colleagues, tutors, and students. He is also guarded in his relationships with male and queer tutors. However, his tension lies in his straight colleagues' perceptions of such interactions, but he notes that it is often straight white male colleagues who have relationships with students, often young white women. Tim also fears how his straight colleagues may perceive his professional relationships with male tutors and students. Tim's fear mirrors Mike's actual campus visit experience, in which future colleagues, without prompting, advised him not to date his students upon his inquiry about campus safety for queer faculty. Tim does not mention any such instance, but such tensions may well link to a Western culture in which queer bodies are and have historically been suspect and policed. Whether affirmed by the Religious Right movement of the late 1970s and early 1980s, or what Michael Warner (1999) calls "moralism," or the Trump administration's transphobic sentiments, straight people have historically had the power to sound alarms at the first sign of supposed queer deviance. In some instances, such queer panic has resulted in any number of queer oppressions—from accusation to violence and imprisonment. All the while, Mike and Tim fear their straight colleague's prospective raised eyebrows, despite academic cultures, pre- and post-#metoo, where straight men and straight women may do the very things of which they accuse and shame queer people.

I pause to comfort nonqueer readers. If you're reading this book, I don't think you're the quintessential oppressor. When I was last a writing center director, I sat in a social justice workshop about antiracism. The facilitator suggested that we, a room made up of mostly white people, avoid statements or even thoughts such as "well, but I'm a good person; I'm not racist." Most of us are good people, and that's not the point. Such claims are dangerous. In moving toward antiracism, these sentiments absolve white people of complicity in inherently racist systems. I learned that such a mindset—one of "we're good people"—sidesteps white complicity in systemic oppression, and further, "good white people" are dangerous because of such complacent mindsets. In the same way I, as a white person of relative privilege, am quite dangerous in adhering to a "good person" narrative in matters of race, I encourage readers not to be upset about how I analyze Tim's and Mike's stories. I feel certain you wouldn't call your colleagues a *fag*, and that you wouldn't assume queer men sleep with their students. But I do not find it productive to ignore the ways straight, supposedly normative people impact queer policing and violence. My statements—and those of this book's participants—may not reflect what you do and who you are. However, there's danger in deeming yourself distant from queer damage. In this sense, I invite you to listen, especially when interacting with participant perspectives like those in this section and this chapter.

Adam describes his former writing center environment, where he was its director in a staff position, as one where he was regularly bullied by colleagues at the neighboring tutoring center, by its leader, and by a student-athletes who filed a false claim about him. His self-described effeminate demeanor and open sexual identity flagged him, he says, much in ways described by Mike. Also, like Mike's experience, it seems Adam's sexuality was just a "pretext" (to use Mike's word) for broader political tensions between his writing center and other institutional forces. For example, Adam's center was located in the Northeast in a private and mostly Left-leaning university. Yet he regularly experienced tensions over territory. Bullies "latched onto" (to use Mike's words again) Adam's sexuality and his effeminacy, which in turn became a focal point—a reason for bullying—for colleagues that called out his sexual orientation due to their discomforts with his writing center site and its political history. Queer people experience this kind of bullying throughout their lives with regularity. We only need to look to school-yards to notice words like *fag* and *faggot* operationalized to violently and homophobically name bodies but also comment on tensions related to conflict, dominance, and toxic masculinity (Pascoe 2007). These instances caused Adam to adopt what he calls a "Joan Crawford" mentality, meaning he was a "bitchy queen" (his words) in order to survive the environment—an environment he eventually departed. He tells me he was supportive of his writing center tutors, often acting as their "mother hen," but had to adopt a tough exterior to interact with his colleagues in the broader university culture.

Jack experiences such straight discourse and bullying as well. His straight male tutor follows his (Jack's) Twitter handle, likely aware he is transgender and tweets about transgender rights. Neither his straight tutor nor Jack were particularly followed on Twitter, hence the likelihood of noticing each other's digital activity, Jack says. Jack recalls being initially jarred by his tutor's quite transphobic tweets, but he resolved the feelings and grew to like his tutor and trust the tutor's writing center work, despite such tweets.

The reality is that experiencing and dealing with this explicit bullying is not merely an offshoot of the work, whether thinking about the stories of Mike, Tim, Adam, or Jack. It is work, as I argue throughout this book. Navigating the minefield that is academia through the world of writing centers, which are often nationally and institutionally misunderstood, is labor in and of itself. Adding "fag" slurs, transphobic tutor tweets, and tensions with straight men and women to the mix is embodied work for bullied, queer administrators. In fact, higher education is ripe with power dynamics that lead to explicit bullying. Shifting academic landscapes and a Western culture in which the long-felt and long-lived privileges of white straight cisgender men are coming into question. Arguably, linked to the #metoo movement and Hollywood's Harvey Weinstein scandal, many of the academy's most historically privileged are seeing those they have oppressed gaining access to what they have always had.

Beyond the #metoo movement's impact on higher education, and perhaps because of the conservative panic it engenders, queer people are targets, plain and simple, and in many ways always have been, despite Western progressive shifts. Western and global cultures, especially under homophobic, transphobic, and populist executive administrations, do not respect or even seek to extend basic rights to queer people, at best; at worst, such administrations and their legacies may contribute to queer and trans deaths. F/X's popular series *Pose* showcases transgender, queer, and drag ballroom cultures of late 1980s and early 1990s Harlem, yet the dominant premise of the telecast is that queer and transgender people of color are always subject to violence, if not death. A similar sentiment prevails in 1990's *Paris Is Burning*, the documentary that spawned *Pose*. For example, *Paris* audiences learn in the film's last frames that Venus Extravaganza, a prominent transgender *Paris* interviewee, was strangled to death, a scenario hauntingly unsurprising to other transgender people in the film, who adopt the sentiment that such is the life of a New York City transgender people of color (Extravaganza 1990).

Such realities exist today. Transgender people are likely to be murdered, as are queer people, even in an age of marriage equality—the touchstone event that often culturally signifies that queer and LGBTQA rights are attained, that fights for human rights are over, and that queer people ought to be happy, settled, and at peace with Western and global landscapes. It was June 2019 in New York City when I first drafted this chapter. I had lived there for just under a year and had been called a *faggot* aggressively by strangers more times than I could count. I was lucky. Recently, a Manhattan lesbian couple was attacked in public transit (Yuhas, *New York Times*, June 7, 2019), while the city's transgender people of color face the same violent landscapes showcased in *Paris* nearly thirty years later (Human Rights Campaign, n.d.). Billy Porter, Broadway sensation and star of F/X's television series *Pose*, alluded to such realities on the afternoon of June 30 during 2019's World Pride event. Showcasing the World Pride parade, three commentators (Porter and two other local New York City anchors) offered four hours of entertaining commentary on the parade, pausing regularly to reflect upon and call viewers to awareness of varied queer phenomena. The commentary was not always uplifting nor only focused on the radical, vibrant, and fabulous one hundred thousand marchers and 3.5 million parade attendees. Porter, a radical queer actor of color of stage and screen, sat front and center, unapologetically and proudly flamboyant, commentating alongside his cohosts, if not in complete leadership of the event. Bespectacled, Porter wore a rainbowed gown by Christian Siriano, a queer designer famous for winning season four of television's *Project Runway*.

On paper, such a scene was a beautiful tribute to the violence of fifty years before at the Stonewall Inn—a bar where New York City queer and trans riots took place on June 28, 1969, which gave rise to the modern gay rights movement. I say "on paper" with hesitation. I do not intend to distract from the magnitude of this event. At thirty-eight years of age, I—a Generation X Texan who came out in 1999, born just after the AIDS crisis advent that haunted American queer men and just when then-President Reagan refused to acknowledge an epidemic—never imagined a world where I would see this happening: a national and local television event hours long and queerly fabulous. I watched with my husband, to whom I had been legally married for nearly ten years. In juxtaposition, Porter paused during the festivities to recognize something to the effect of "this parade is wonderful, but the fight is not over." Porter and other commentators paused to reflect, asking a question to the rhythm of "How many transgender deaths have there been this year? Five or six?" Clearly, the hosts were in hour three of a live telecast; they did not have access to statistics, nor were they called upon or hired to comment in those specific terms. I do not blame them for this fumble. "Five or six" was, perhaps, the number just for New York City's Manhattan, as the national numbers far exceed single digits, with the Human Rights Campaign reporting that 2017 and 2018 saw twenty-nine and twenty-six transgender deaths from acts of violence, respectively (Human Rights Campaign, n.d.). The number for transgender violence that does not end in fatality is likely exponentially higher, which is to say that even in a world where a queer celebrity of color adorned with rainbow garb is lead commentator for a televised World Pride parade, the fight is not over, as many have said, including Porter, and as many more will say.

Nonqueer writing center practitioners may gasp at the homophobic epithets, at the fear felt by Black queer writing center directors, and at the transphobic tweets directed at a transgender writing center director discussed in this chapter. They may also wince or roll their eyes at my suggested link between explicit bullying, queer death, and writing centers. That we know of, a queer person has not been killed in a writing center. Yet I would be surprised if queer writing center practitioners reading this section would blink an eye. They may have even seen in the world or on the job some of the very things, minus perhaps explicit violence, taking place in their own centers. Denny (2011) and Denny et al. (2019) remind practitioners that the world plays out in our writing centers, especially in sites that house one-to-one human interaction. As Hallman Martini and Webster (2017b) suggest, bravery, not safety, is a writing center's only survival vehicle for its stakeholders. If we take Denny and company, Hallman Martini, and Webster to heart, the work of writing centers in the twenty-first century may very well be haunted by such queer violence, with immense impact on workers who cannot easily ignore the news or turn a blind eye when their own bodies are intertwined, implicated, and invoked by such violence. In a world where queer people can be beaten or shot at random in public places, it is not a stretch to say that the bravery theories of recent writing center research put metaphorical and material weight on and within the professional lives of writing center workers.

TENSIONS: IMPLICIT BULLYING

While not called names, nor explicitly feared, many participants note colleagues' passive aggressions and cognitive dissonances while acting otherwise as supportive peers. Brian expresses tension with how he was perceived in his previous writing center directorship: as a "big scary gay black writing center director." The narrative of the nurturing, feminized, white leader is not "how [he] was taught that writing centers operate and function" when he was first a writing tutor at an HBCU, as he tells us in a previous chapter. Brian is not necessarily bullied in the traditional sense: his race and his size ("muscular," as he describes himself) afford him much in the way of avoiding bullying (though certainly the question of physicality and its relationship to bullying doesn't have an easy answer). Yet, he is nearly the only professional of color at his university, whether faculty or staff. Like other Black queer participants, hushed side conversations craft a narrative of his writing center director identity: the word "scary," as he says, is often the first and foremost qualifier. A hushed underlife surrounds his queer administration, which despite such local mythologies, does not hold weight: at the time of this project, he was active in the writing center field, often collaborating with his tutors and encouraging them to attend the field's major conferences, like the

International Writing Centers Association (IWCA). He often houses the only Black-oriented campus communities, which is to say that the few Black people on campus, whether faculty, staff, or students, tend to gravitate to his writing center to find community. Brian nurtures, for lack of a better term, that environment, despite being supposedly "big and scary."

James is also a queer man of color, and his colleagues are "fine with it," he tells me, suggesting his sexuality is not an issue at his writing center nor at his institution, minus the under-the-radar tensions he occasionally has with a hypermasculine, exveteran colleague. James describes a Black queer physicality he feels impacts how university stakeholders view his writing center and its administration, so much so that he wonders aloud to me about a recent decrease in writing center appointment numbers. Like Brian, James describes his physique as fit and muscular. He is someone who works out regularly, he tells me, implying he might be less likely to be bullied. His thinking points to the underlife of queer administrators and its felt impact on their work. The bullying energy generated around fear of and false narratives of Black queer administration does, indeed, impact the work of these Black queer administrators, and ultimately is labor, as articulated in this chapter. These Black men describe an underlife to their writing center administrations, which is distinct from the queer white people of this book, in particular the queer white men. While Mike, Tim, Adam, and Jack, all white male participants, experience textbook bullying, targeting, and mobbing, the black queer men of this study seemed to be feared for their large physiques and Black bodies—a historically racist association that dates back at least a few hundred years in Western cultures. It would be difficult to parse out the lesser of evils of either outside perception. On one hand, these Black queer writing center directors are not the subject of the same kinds of bullying as these white men. Their masculine, perhaps "passing," bodies save them from particular forms of explicit bullying; however, implicit fear and erasure also impact these Black men. For example, Brian's writing center tutoring course often doesn't fill (though it does fill, he tells me, when a white woman teaches it), while James, above, worries aloud about appointment numbers and cancellations as they relate to this Black queer physique. For the writing center practitioners in this study, the relationship between bullying and labor is complex: white participants' concerns surround harm to their physical bodies, while Black participants worry about their feared bodies' impact on their centers' performances. Neither situation is tenable.

Like Brian and James, Stephanie also fears that a hushed underlife surrounds her writing center administration; she wonders, given what she overhears, what is said in her absence. Stephanie's colleagues are supportive of her, though as she passed through a campus dining hall, she overheard a straight colleagues' verbalized support of antigay legislation in her southern state. She articulates discomfort with how otherwise supportive colleagues can separate her from the larger landscape. They support and like her but would essentially vote against her best interests. Alongside this tension, Stephanie's gender nonconforming physicality may impact her recruitment of tutors, she says, as she wonders about the possibilities for tutor recruitment if she were slightly more conforming.

Slightly less implicit, but still grounded in an underlife, Madeline's evangelical tutors and colleagues invited her to church regularly when she first took on her writing center directorship in the South. Laughingly, she tells me she took this gesture as especially kind at first, thinking they were trying to invite her into their community. She pauses to tell me something I'm familiar with as a person from the South: inviting queer people to church or offering to pray for them is often a paternalistic gesture implying dissatisfaction with a queer person's sexuality. Such is part of the "polite veneer of the south," she tells me, a statement I understand well, having grown up and lived much of my life in southeast Texas.

Loaded politeness impacts Leah as well. While she was participating in a safe-space training at her institution, her white straight male colleague took part in an activity in which he was able to imply he actually spends a great deal of time with queer people and that his closer relationships are with queer people. Leah's results for the activity showed just the opposite, and she even jokes, somewhat nervously, that her test preferences implied she exhibits internalized homophobia "against [herself] in some way," despite her lived experiences that point to self-actualized realities. Per an interaction in which the "woke man" mansplained, however politely, to her just how "woke" he is and how much of an ally he is to the local queer community, she laughs and says to me about him: "Well, good for you." I laugh knowingly, having heard similar sentiments from straight people. In this case, queer people are not trusted to understand their own interpersonal relationships, supposedly needing straight woke white people to teach them about queer relationships and internalized homophobia.

Along these lines, Jennifer, who holds a more precarious professional position, talks about her experiences with direct tensions coming out at writing centers in both the South and the Northeast. In fact, she dreaded disclosing her lesbian identity to her boss in the Northeast. Her boss's response: "I couldn't fire you if I wanted to." As we talk, Jennifer nervously laughs a bit at that response; I find it a bit jarring. Having had to come out myself many times at many institutions across the United States, I know well-intentioned superiors occasionally mutter statements that come across awkwardly, yet the modal verbs used by her supervisor imply rhetorical conditions.

At worst, participants are called "fags" and "scary" Black people and tweeted at transphobically; at best, they are subject to passive-aggressive statements or imposed, fictionalized underlives crafted and mythologized around their writing center administrations alongside occasional, unwarranted prayer and awkward invitations to church. They face colleagues who are "fine with it," who are paternalistic ("I'm more actually more queer-friendly than you are!"), and who offer conditional statements or jokes about job terminations. Being a queer writing center director in the twenty-first century is not being a homeless transgender person of color. It is not a snapshot into the violent queer assaults that continue to plague urban cities and rural sites across the United States. It is not being removed from your home because of being queer or trans. Yet participant responses tiptoe hauntingly around the national conversation about queer job termination, which corroborates Hallman Martini and Webster's (2017b) claim that writing center work requires bravery in its stakeholders. In a landscape where writing center practitioners, like me, write about queer issues from tenure-stream or tenured privileged positions, and where a recent International Writing Centers conference's (2018) theme was activism and bodies, queer writing center directors, despite many holding established positions, may still face job insecurity. And such professional insecurity may still pose difficulties even in a national landscape where the Supreme Court of the United States recently ruled queer and transgender work-based discrimination unconstitutional, as work-based discrimination doesn't necessary disappear with SCOTUS rulings; it may just go under the radar, hiding in instances that "you can't put your finger on," as James, a queer participant of color, reminds us earlier in this chapter.

We, as a Western and global culture, are not past certain lived realities for queer people. Similarly, one participant has published about his experiences with explicit homophobia that took place during his undergraduate tutoring years. These experiences took place and were published in the late 1980s and early 1990s, yet Amanda, another participant, describes similar instances that took place in the mid-2000s. As relevant writing center research about identity work suggests, the writing center, for these practitioners, is the "messy" world (Dixon 2017) of the outside. Drawing upon Denny (2010) and Anne Ellen Geller, Michele Eodice, Frankie Condon, Meg Carroll, and Elizabeth Boquet (2007),

Elise Dixon (2017) reminds writing center laborers that the intersection, and ultimately perfect storm, of queerness and messiness often collide in the writing center for its stakeholders. These messy possibilities create work environments for the participants of this study that, as stated through this text, are in actuality work. As I argue throughout this book, the embodied experiences of these queer practitioners extend beyond the writing center field's current disciplinary language for naming such work. *Emotional labor* (Caswell, Grutsch McKinney, and Jackson 2016) doesn't quite cut it in that this work extends beyond "care, mentoring, and nurturing" and far beyond "resolving conflicts" and simply "managing display of emotion" (27). And, while Denny and Geller (2013) offer a disciplinary lens for understanding relationships among and repercussions of writing center work and research production, such attention is a mere tributary of the larger systemic body of occurrences. How the labor of being bullied impacts participant research is critical, sure, but matters less in the grand scheme. Does it matter that being called a *fag* or fearing being fired for being an out queer impacts research productivity? Certainly it does, and certainly if practitioners published more and pulled back on the activism of the previous chapter (i.e., the invisible CVs), professional mobility would prospectively afford them different professional avenues and environments. But is that the point? The unstated job descriptions of writing center work may impact these participants' research productivity, but that disciplinary framework sidesteps the systemic framework of the realities of the labor; it is a Band-Aid on a gunshot wound to the chest. These participant stories, however, offer writing center researchers new stories, new language, and new ways of understanding the labor of writing center administration in a queer body. Being bullied, whether explicitly or implicitly, whether biting and outwardly caustic or marginally or passively aggressively understated, is rather exhausting work imposed upon these participants.

TENSIONS: DENIAL OF WELCOME, ERASURE, AND (DIFFICULTY) LANDING POSITIONS IN THE DISCIPLINE

Brian is leaving the writing center field. "People like me are not part of the conversation," he says. He explains that queer, cisgender, and white male administrators do indeed fall in line with mainstream writing center director administrative perspectives but once again notes how mainstream writing center pedagogies fail to recognize HBCU writing center administrative pedagogies, especially those that framed his earlier orientation to writing center leadership and practice. Brian's thoughts about absence and erasure are corroborated by recent writing center research. In *Praxis: A Writing Center Journal*'s 2019 special issue "Race and the Writing Center" (Riddick and Hooker 2019), the eight articles represent much of the race-based writing center scholarship of the past decade, stemming perhaps from the work of Laura Greenfield and Karen Rowan (2011), two white scholars who call for further research on race, and just a few other articles written by people of color (Faison and Trevino 2017) that explicitly deal with writing centers and race. And of this special issue, just three articles intersect with queer issues, while just one explicitly theorizes the intersection of race and queerness (Lockett 2019). Brian explains that he would, in fact, love to see an empirical project on queer Black male tutors, as the "narratives [of writing center work] would be so much different than what people are used to hearing," suggesting a chasm between Black and queer voices and topics and voices and topics privileged in writing center research of past and present.

Brian calls out this research chasm. But like many academic administrators of color, he is exhausted. So much so that, as this study concluded, he left the writing center field, focusing primary on another research area. His departure points quite specifically to retention, of course. We as a discipline clearly do not retain professionals of color. But further, Brian's departure points to the research lost and the perspectives absent when queer Black practitioners depart the writing center world. At the time of this book's conclusion, only a few projects had surfaced that showcase the research and voices of queer people of color, such as the work of Wonderful Faison and Willow Trevino (2017).

Landing writing center positions is not without tensions for queer and raced bodies. Amanda found that securing a writing center position with her gender nonconforming gender presentation was, at first, a bit frightening. Would her "boyish haircut" pose problems for her? It did not, she tells me. In fact, she finds the writing center field to be among the most queer-friendly fields she can image, one in which queer theories and progressive politics reign. She remembers holding a copy of Denny's *Writing Center Journal* article "Queering the Writing Center" as she was about to start rhetoric and composition graduate work, feeling at ease that such an article existed in her chosen field. Amanda's position on the writing center field is quite common, in fact, as the discipline is certainly, at face value, queer friendly. Conversely, Madeline, another participant, tells me about a queer scholar for whom the job search was not so seamless and friendly. The queer candidate was later privy to inside jokes and explicitly derogatory remarks about his effeminate demeanor while on campus. An insider warned him about these back-channel conversations. Madeline did not delve into that story in detail, thus it would difficult to offer much beyond speculation about this insider.

While no participant explicitly discussed experiences with homophobic or transphobic hiring committees themselves, participants either disclosed past fears or recounted violences against other candidates on the academic job market. As Jeremy tells us in the opening of this chapter, a Trump rally took place just before his campus visit for a tenure-track writing center position, and a student of color was murdered around the same time, which was quite haunting for him. Caroline Dadas (2013, 2018) and Jennifer Sano-Franchini (2016) warn us about the broader rhetoric and composition field's job-market realities for people of intersectional difference, namely queer people. While such scholarship does not include discussion of a post-Trump-election hiring landscape, the landscape of which participants speak in this project, the research holds. My 2015 job talk for a writing center position, for which I opened with an anecdote about my husband, elicited audible gasps from the audience at my former Houston institution. A tutor who attended my research talk and later worked at the writing center site I was hired to direct told me in so many words that I was brave. He said, "Wow, [you] did not give a sh—what people thought" and that I "was fearless" when deciding to refer to my husband during a campus-wide job presentation. On one hand, I was delighted and honored to hear such a statement. On the other, my mind eventually returned to those audible gasps and the realities of being an out queer person on the rhetoric and composition job market. Despite the stories we in our discipline—and ultimately, higher education—may tell ourselves, the reality is that a mere six years ago, intentionally and purposefully referring to my husband during a job talk was radical for many in attendance. I got the job. At the time, as a job candidate, I held many privileges: I was transitioning from a postdoctoral fellowship at a research-intensive site with two openly gay, generous, and compassionate rhetoric and composition mentors. There, I had a generous salary in the area I grew up in with a working spouse while I job searched. This decision to disclose a same-sex spouse during a job talk was strategic but also stacked with privilege in that I could have not gotten the job and survived. Many queer practitioners are not so privileged; in a recent job-market year, fewer than ten tenure-stream, noncontingent writing center directorships were posted in our discipline's job-circulation venues (Ridolfo 2019).

Once participants secure jobs, the landscape itself may exclude them, as Brian aptly reminds us in his message to the field about its disciplinary and empirical gaps in research. Such realities, in some way, make the job-market discussion moot in that the field may not even be able to recruit the voices, those of queer people of color, from whom it could learn the most. Even this project's participant pool is lacking in that it is indeed very queer but is not intersectionally raced, as I account for in the methods section. Several questions arise: for example, What might the fact that there are no queer women of color in the project tell us? It may speak to my recruitment methods in that despite my best intentions, especially through direct recruitment of two men of color, I was still not able to secure the participation of even one queer woman of color. I recruited at two national conferences, on the queer writing center listserv through the IWCA SIG, and through participants, peers, and mentors. Despite fabulous queer graduate students of color rising through the writing center ranks, no one could name a queer woman of color in a writing center directorship while I was recruiting participants. Is this an issue of safety and trust that links back to Brian's attention to the scarcities in queer-of-color writing center voices and perspectives in research? Is this issue also linked to disciplinary erasures in that queer women of color in particular (though, we certainly don't see many queer Black male writing center voices showcased) are not included in the discipline much, if at all? Further, do issues of disciplinary access plague queer women of color in writing centers in that even national calls or attentive snowball sampling does not create a vehicle for offering such women platforms for research participation? The answer to these questions is yes, I'm certain. To echo Elder and Davila's (2019) claim that those who experience oppression in the world writ large also experience it in their jobs, such a reality is present even in this study, simply perhaps due to a perfect storm of recruitment, retention, access, and trust. Beyond the conventional parameters of writing center work, the weight of a national landscape rife with violent tension cannot be separated from our work sites, as we see in this book—*Pulse*, Tyler Clementi, and homophobic and transphobic slurs have all interfaced with queer writing center work, as the next section will showcase.

TENSIONS: NATIONAL ZEITGEIST

This section ties to this book's activism chapter in that national events often signal queer people to act in particularly justice-motivated ways.

As the previous chapter delves into, national events elicited responses from participants, and these activisms did lead to fear. With this said, participants also express tensions about such national events without any inclination to respond to such events in particular ways. They are human, and despite disciplinary and institutional pressure to respond in culturally connected ways, often the tension surrounding the event, not any sort of activism, is the primary labor.

As mentioned in this chapter's historical vignettes, Jeremy campus-visited at his site just after a Trump rally during the 2016 election season. A student of color was murdered during the same time frame. Out and proud during his job talk, he felt tension around his out queer identity and the prospect of taking the job, despite his university's queer-friendly environment, much like the story I offered about my own experience in the previous section. Simply the proximity to hate speech and hate crimes was enough for Jeremy to take a pause in his experience on campus. He was drawn to the position because of its established, reputable writing center and its proximity to his family, though he did hesitate, laboring around the tension of taking a job in such an environment. The ghosts of this known event haunting his transition to a new tenure-track writing center directorship is, first and foremost, its own labor, perhaps somewhere between emotional and invisible, though not easily identified alongside or within those terms. Local violence may impact any compassionate practitioner, though in a national landscape in which former President Trump acknowledged national and world Pride events while tweeting homophobic and transphobic statements, Jeremy's tension and discomfort as a queer person were nuanced. But Jeremy grew to find a home at his current institution. Early in his tenure, he posted to social media just how accepting the environment is, by uploading a picture of a university-wide, queer-friendly residential housing initiative. I point to Jeremy's story and landscape to note also that "ghosts," as Mike calls them, and energies may haunt queer administrators' sites. "Ghosts" may take the form of previous administrators, as they do in Mike's case, but may also connote events, like the ones Jeremy describes. Institutional ethnography research in the writing center and rhetoric and composition field (LaFrance 2019; LaFrance and Nicolas 2012; Miley 2017) suggests that programs, sites, and, ultimately and especially, people are impacted by the varied networks, cultures, and human and nonhuman factors mapped onto spaces, which is to say all the rainbow flags on campus still may not be enough to erase Jeremy's memories mapped to being a queer job candidate for his center during a time of homophobic and political unrest. The 2016 election cycle still haunts many of us, but I argue it especially resonates with people of color, queer and transgender people, and those whose identities intersect. Such memories, simply for his recounting them for his interview for this book, speak to how his labor was impacted by these events at various stages—from the campus visit through his early writing center administration. As practitioners, we cannot simply cast aside the prospective impact of homophobic "ghosts" upon the work of these queer laborers. These events and Jeremy's work comingle hauntingly.

The Trump era's posttruth rhetorics (McComiskey 2017) impact Jack as well. He tells me that since transitioning, his male body at his administrative site, on occasion, elicits tensions for him. "I look like a middle-aged white guy," he tells me of his female-to-male gender transition. He goes on to say he worries about the impact his body may have in his space and institution. He sees it, as he recounts in this book's activism chapter, as a space where people can learn from him about compassion but also struggles with it when working with international students who may perceive the current Trump administration as a threat to their national citizenship status, as deportation is a major action of the administration. On occasion, Jack wonders if he passes as a cisgender straight white male to a fault in that his male body may have less pedagogical leverage for teaching in some contexts. He tells me a story about an international student he worked with who disclosed that he learned in a STEM course that when people have gender reassignment surgeries, they "mutilate their bodies." Jack feels tense about this statement for many reasons: (1) the colleague who may be teaching this transphobic curriculum and its intersection with the writing center, its tutors, and Jack's lived experiences, (2) the student who may be misinterpreting the curriculum and transphobically translating the instructor's words, and (3) Jack's prospective passing as the "middle-aged white guy," thus creating dynamics in which the passing signals others to offer transphobic sentiments, however innocent or grounded in misunderstanding such statements may be. The Trump administration played a role in his fear. In situations discussed in other chapters, we can see Jack is quick to act. In this instance, he stayed silent, he tells me. He perhaps felt defeated and deflated as a transgender worker whose labor intersects with the transphobia of the current administration.

The previous chapter points to instances in which participants felt an inherent desire, calling, or pressure to respond with activist intent to national events from their queer leadership and writing center sites—that is, administrative action, whether visible, invisible, traditionally work based, or personally and politically linked—to make, signal, or work toward cultural or global change. But not all participants necessarily linked this work to a local, global, or glocal work-based phenomenon. Sometimes, the experiences were, well, tense and uncomfortable and did not warrant taking action, per se. Elder and Davila's (2019) collection, for example, and a long history of rhetoric and composition scholarship, points to problematic working conditions, instances, and interactions without any sort of didactic, instructive, or pedagogical framework for responding in activist ways to the work. In this sense, this section points to instances in which participants just felt the tension. The previous chapter suggests queer people ought to use tension around national events to do something, especially in terms of making change, but such pressure is quite unfair and unbalanced.

CONCLUSION

In a recent summer Rhetoric Society of America Institute, Jackie Rhodes, during a cofacilitated workshop with Jonathan Alexander (2019), reminded attendees that pain is part of queer life—integral to it, in fact, which I reference in a previous chapter. In returning to her claims, pain leads to growth, to evolution, and to new queer worlds where we, as queer people, can imagine and gravitate toward new lived possibilities from our progressive, radical action. From this vantage point, work itself may be metaphorically, if not materially, painful. When we labor, we worry, we fear, we feel anxiety, we care, and we act in our administrative spaces, whether we are queer or not. Such pain is part of the work landscape. Rhodes (Rhodes and Alexander 2019) complicates this notion, arguing that queer pain that extends from violence is a different kind of animal, unwarranted and embodied, wherein ghosts of inflicted violence impede and stifle growth. Yet this growth, this queer worldmaking, isn't possible when, for example, queer writing center practitioners are bullied, mobbed, and subjected to aggressions in the work spaces they lead. Homophobic slurs and transphobic sentiments make productive and fulfilling work lives impossible. While such instances are not physically violent acts against queer people that pervade global cultures, such actions imposed by others are not without consequence to queer workers. The emotional weight of coming out (Eliot 1996), of being subject to slurs, or of knowing colleagues smile to your face and vote against you in local and national elections is more than just emotional labor, more than mere invisible work; it is part of the administrative work for queer people. It is, in fact, work. Mustering the nerve to head to campus to face colleagues who call you a fag is work. Monitoring your facial expressions while overhearing hushed homophobic political sentiments and knowing your colleagues operationalize cognitive dissonance when distinguishing between you and less acceptable immaterial queers who exist in the fantasy of Western media is work, always.

Bullying acts are on a sliding scale. Not every instance is a slur nor a moment of passive aggression. A queer single man, David reflects upon imbalanced workloads for single queer people without children and points to habitual passive aggression from his colleagues, even if many of them are mostly well intentioned and queer friendly. Collegial assumptions about coworkers whose lives do not align heteronormatively can lead to queer people taking on the brunt of departmental service. Such imbalance posits a set of assumptions about queer lives, especially that queer people have less rigorous personal lives and can thus, as the narrative might go, take on departmental service in ways that straight colleagues with children supposedly can't. While, as argued in previous chapters, this work isn't part of a job description, it is indeed invisible labor that extends beyond a CV. We as practitioners, especially in the writing center world, often assume labor at work is exerted for purposes of productivity, something that propels forward an organized body or entity. To hold the disciplinary values we say we do, especially in the writing center world, where identity, intersectionality, justice, and radicalism guide our sites, we must to listen to, hear, and understand the realities of the landscapes. These stories must live in spaces beyond hearsay and lore. An empirical glimpse is necessary, as the field has often told stories but little exists that blends narrative, empiricism, and analysis. The following section seeks to offer a final grounding for this conversation.

Queer writing center directors are bullied pre- and posttenure, disrupting cross-disciplinary lore that the field's most professionally vulnerable and most bullied are predominantly pretenure faculty members or staff. The bullying takes place across the country, not only in particular regions.

That writing center directors are bullied is not necessarily news. Elder and Davila (2019) make this claim, as do others (Denny 2014) in recent rhetoric and composition and writing center research. Many of those who report bullying in this chapter were tenured faculty members with administrative appointments. Granted, some bullying took place before tenure, but that academic standing did not protect queer writing center directors from it. And many who did not report bullying held staff positions, sometimes in regions of the country not historically associated with peace for queer people—the South, for example. On one hand, such omission may point to participant discomfort, but that seems unlikely given that this project's most "out and proud," so to speak, said little about bullying, and many of those participants were from the South and the oft-conservative Midwest. Further, Mike's and Adam's explicit bullying took place on the East Coast, which is, on paper, among the most supposedly "queer friendly" regions represented in this book. Yet, such coastal peace did not hold up along in the face of these queer writing center directors' experiences.

Queer bullying resembles what people of color may face as writing center directors.
   Such comparable bullying is not an exact representation, but it certainly rhymes. And for those queer directors of color in this project, the bullying may be implicit but is no less jarring, which in these cases has led to retention and ultimately recruitment issues in the writing center discipline. However, the bullying of queer people and of people of color does differ. A hostility exists in queer participant experiences, whereas a veiled politeness seems to pervade many of the stories of rhetoric and composition administrators of color. The word *fag* directed at Mike and the instances of explicit bullying related to particular slurs have not been discussed in empirical research in the writing center field thus far. And people of color may certainly experience slurs in writing centers, though empirical research has not yet unveiled it (but perhaps it should, as Brian suggests when he notes that writing center research has not necessarily delved rigorously into Black writing center practitioner experience). This section is certainly complicated by the experiences of two participants of color in that they have queer and raced bodies. As Crenshaw (1991, 2018) teaches us, we cannot reduce a person to a single identity, for our selves are intersectionally woven. In this sense, neither person of color noted explicit bullying because of their queerness, yet both mentioned at least implicit bullying related to their Black identities, especially in disciplinary erasure.

The majority of queer administrators reported that bullying takes place implicitly.
   Mike's, Jack's, and Adam's explicit homophobic and transphobic experiences were explicit, but most bullying takes place under the radar—in hushed whispers, in unstated but implicit sentiments. This chapter's distinction between explicit and implicit bullying is limiting, for certain, in that a slur is its own kind of violence, though the slow stabs of passive aggression are no less trying, no less violent for these queer administrators. While Mike was called a *fag* and Jack experienced transphobia on Twitter, not all such participant instances were as "in your face." These slow, methodical stabs at queer administrators are,

perhaps, just as violent as explicit bullying. The deep wound of a slur causes immediately and embodied impact, whereas a million under-the-table cuts cause a bleeding out, so to speak.

Bullying takes its toll on these participant laborers and also may impact the merit, production, and sustainability of the writing center discipline.

David, who is overworked as his department's only single, queer man, told me stories of his workload. At face value, a workload is perhaps not a form of bullying, yet it can point to how repeated, long-term privileging of workplace heteronormativity impacts queer practitioners. David says that, at his institution, queer administrators in general are given bigger workloads, a practice stemming from the assumption that they don't have nuclear families with children and that they have more time and resources. When queer families or queer people without families are subject to unbalanced administrative and departmental work, decisions are being made, however intentioned, about the distribution of labor. With this distribution in mind, I return to Brian, who questions why, at this point in time, particular kinds of Black queer writing center research have not yet emerged in the discipline. The impact of bullying, even the ways it may transpire in queer workload distribution, could indeed tango with the realities of research projects that still have not surfaced in the discipline. Brian is flabbergasted that a project about young queer Black tutors hasn't come to fruition. Similarly, this project itself, despite the fact that the first issue of *The Writing Center Journal* was published in 1980 (i.e., a writing center research history that dates back nearly forty years), seems as if it could have been taken up long before my entry into the field. Readers may question the relationship between queer bullying and queer research production, but many disciplinary realities dictate the kinds of research that surface in modern writing center work. If we value Geller and Denny's (2013) claims that writing center labor must always already be linked to a research identity for both the sustainability and credibility of the discipline, as well its practitioners, then we as a field must listen carefully to these stories that trace relationships among queer bullying, labor, and production (a discussion that takes more extensive form in this book's conclusion). Nearly monthly, we hear of yet another writing center overtaken by upper administration, if not reassigned to another university unit or closed for business. Within this landscape, our continued establishment of a discipline, our very livelihood and sustainability, rests upon positioning ourselves as a research-based, dynamic discipline led by intersectionally diverse stakeholders. Our queer and of color practitioners are telling us to listen and to act through recruitment, retention, and research. What queer and raced research projects may lie dormant due to an imbalance of labor experienced by queer practitioners?

This empirical glimpse, which aligns in some ways with replicable, aggregable, and data-driven (RAD) work, may suggest generalizability in the relationship between the on-the-job bullying and research production. Yet to counter the argument for RAD writing center research, generalizability may be moot in this case, as ultimately who cares whether the data is generalizable? From a methodological standpoint, the methods are replicable. But even one iota of empirical evidence that suggests the bullying of queer practitioners ought to make writing center practitioners listen up. Nonqueer writing center administrators could be better allies and accomplices not by questioning these relationships, nor focusing on generalizability, but by listening to the queer participant perspectives, recognizing that twelve of twenty participants volunteered experiences with some form of bullying, with many directly linking the experiences to their work loads and their research production.

More broadly, participants experienced tensions as queer administrators around national events. When juxtaposed with the previous chapter's discussions about the relationship between activism and national events, this chapter's empirical glimpses differ. Many participants simply felt tensions, without the need to act upon how this tension informed events. When further juxtaposed with the disciplinary pressures unpacked in the previous chapter, perhaps the most strategic maneuvers for disciplinary sustainability involve not more events- and mission-based activism, which Hallman Martini (2018) calls into question, but more research. The activism discussed in this book often takes particular forms unrecognizable to the discipline and difficult to align with shared parameters for knowledge advancement. Is the answer to channel this tension into research rather than toward the pressure to be social justice activists? Put another way, so as to account for the ways research production is activism, should our calling be away from parade marching, mission-statement writing, and events-based organizing to publishing about our field—such as initiating more projects that provide empirical glimpses into justice, equity, inclusion, and identity. A dearth of empirical research in areas related to identity is quite telling.

PARTING WORDS

Navigating institutional and disciplinary tensions is work, not a mere consequence or implication of it. Further, the work, to follow this book's labor framework, is indeed laborious. And invisible. Where does one "count" such work? Where and how does a queer worker document administrative survival, at worst, and at best awkward or tense interactions? This type of exhausting and trying work also impacts other work, critical to queer administrators' professional development and long-term livelihood—such as their capacities for writing center research and disciplinary participation. Yet these workers push through, for better or for worse. From this vantage point, queer practitioners offer us untapped queer perspectives that provide the writing center field with dynamic, fresh repertoires that may better sustain and foster the discipline in an age when writing centers close regularly and nationally. This book's next chapter—its conclusion—continues to speak to how participant voices across capital, activism, and tension may help us understand our work in writing center and writing studies administration.

5
CONCLUSION

This book is an effort to think about the intersection of queer identity and writing center labor. I, with support from and conversations with twenty fabulous queer writing center directors, attempt to answer research questions about naming what queer writing center administrative labor looks like, about what happens when queer people direct writing centers, and about what these people, perspectives, and dynamics mean for the writing center discipline. The book suggests, from many vantage points, that queer writing center labor—that is, work done by queer people in writing center administrative positions—is distinct and nuanced in that it differs as often as it aligns with what we talk about in the discipline when we talk about writing center work.

I can't speak for every way these practitioners do their work and labor on behalf of their sites, nor can I say with certainly that every labored instance is immediately and specifically wrapped up in and implicated by these queer identities. What I can say is that, across twenty extensive discussions, queer-participant perspectives led to distinct meaning-making for and alongside writing center work. I have written this book with the understanding that most of my readers are not queer people. Two of my closest colleagues reminded me, politely, directively, and rightly, that I should write with the intent to speak to nonqueer readers as often as queer ones. Much of this book will spark queer readers to nod their head as they recall side conversations, listserv discussions, and special-interest groups at our regional and national organizations' conferences, especially in terms of claims that have up to this point existed primarily in our field's lore. In this sense, an empirical, date-driven glimpse into queer work life was necessary at this moment. Lore isn't so bad, of course; it's part of the life of writing centers. Yet as I worked through this project with these queer folks, I did imagine that a data-focused approach would help many practitioners across many sexual orientations trace these long-suspected realities that have existed mostly as undocumented conversations in informal settings.

DOI: 10.7330/9781646421497.c005

LEARNING FROM QUEER CAPITAL

Our queer colleagues draw upon distinct queer histories, not always bright and cheery but always salient and relevant, that help them lead their writing center sites. In this sense, history matters for how and why we do our work in writing centers, whether queer or straight. A capital that functions much like an administrative queer literacy surfaces as participants do their work. Nearly all participants spoke to such capacities. Queer origins and rhetorical readiness offered a framework for understanding this queer capital. Capital, much like queer labor, is a relatively unexamined area in writing center studies, at least as it interfaces with labor, work, and jobs, and certainly as these elements are made complex through queer lenses. The participant work performed and the embodied histories and capacities (i.e., capital) inherent in these queer people speak to a distinct paradox: this book's queer writing center directors are regarded, rightly so, as queer diversity unicorns always equipped for writing center labor. Their institutions, writing centers, tutors, students, and colleagues understand them as such; they themselves may embrace wearing this hat. Yet, the book's narrative arc into activism and tension teaches us that readiness, aptitude, and willingness for particular kinds of work differentially position these workers at their sites and in the broader discipline.

LEARNING FROM QUEER ACTIVISM

Our queer colleagues do activist work—there's not another name for it—like helping tutors through trauma, like proactive support for mental and sexual health. They often gravitate toward this work, in fact. It often drives and is integrated in their administrative labor. Field leaders and major writing center sites support this disciplinary grounding. Rhetoric and composition doctoral programs at universities like Michigan State University (MSU) and Purdue University offer graduate-level writing center courses framed in such topics. A glance at the writing center page on MSU's website showcases a beautiful mission statement alluding to a queer pedagogy and vision. It offers audiences and stakeholders a glimpse into the work of the writing center grounded in the traditional day-to-day labor (i.e., they consult on writing, they offer workshops) while also naming their work alongside identity rhetorics and social justice. At the time of this study, both MSU leaders were out lesbians who integrated queer themes of activism, justice, and equity into everything from their graduate and undergraduate training courses to their site-based research and physical spaces and satellites. The

Purdue University Writing Lab is led by an out gay man whose research across his published work focuses on queer theory and its application to writing center tutorials, as well as qualitative studies of the writing center world, many of which are identity based. Our most prominent sites to which we look for guidance and cutting-edge administration and pedagogy are led often by queer writing center directors. We can only thank these queer leaders for this work and this inspiration; its legacy is vast in the writing center discipline's gravitation toward social justice and its theoretical and quotidian implications.

As stated in this book's activism chapter, this kind of work may be less tumultuous for people like Madeline and Mike, both of whom hold secure, tenured writing center directorships at research-intensive universities. Madeline's makes it possible to "roll right over" any tensions she might face; some of her confidence stems from her personality (she tends to diffuse tense situations with her "lesbian humor," as she calls it). However, many participants who hold at-will or non-tenure-stream directorships are just as out, just as forthright, and just as "activist" in their work, such as Stephanie's positions in the South in staff and at-will positions, and Dana's, Casey's, and Amanda's work in rural areas. In fact, many of this book's most "out and proud" in their administrative approaches live and work in the South, a far cry from narratives that suggest queers, queerness, and queer activisms take place only in urban centers in coastal regions.

Where participants work complicates the disciplinary conversations about what kind of writing center leadership is possible in what regions of the country. Yet, the fact that this activist work often falls on queer practitioners is one of the most notable and glaring double-edged swords of this book. Queer workers are drawn to this work, they observe and respect queer writing center leaders, like those at Michigan State University and Purdue University who do such work. And queer workers are, perhaps, most equipped for it, alongside queer colleagues of color and straight men and women of color, as students with queer identities enter colleges to study, work, and write at exponential and unprecedented rates. Participants discuss labor that, quite literally, could save lives through mental- and sexual-health advocacy; through being go-to queer mentors to countless queer and transgender tutors; and through holding space regularly for queer and of color tutors, colleagues, and students at their universities. But the labor named and analyzed in this book is still labor. It is both invigorating and trying, if not regularly traumatic, for these queer workers. Higher education creeps toward regular conversations—even tailored advice—about faculty and administrative burnout (Daniel 2020; Goodblar 2018). Surprisingly, this word did not come up in participant discussions, despite narratives that could point to such labor conditions. With this said, participants did regularly discuss setting boundaries around the queer components of their administration, especially related to queer tutor and student support. Not that these queer mentees were a burden upon these participants; quite the opposite, it was this work that nearly all participants recounted with pride. However, the work (again, emphasis on the word *work*) could be taxing. Participants noted that an intensity around open-door policies or queer students seeking them out for support elicited boundary setting. They occasionally closed their doors or left campus early campus, fully intent on returning the next day to show up for this kind of queer labor. But first: rest.

Along these lines, a queer senior colleague, who didn't participate in the project, once said to me, in jest, "Writing center directors are too busy complaining about their work, or being activists, to do much research." Such a statement is a tongue-in-cheek but sobering exaggeration and, on occasion, a disciplinary reality, which is to say that research, as a proper and explicit topic, came up very little in participant discussions, despite interview questions that specifically led to avenues where it could be discussed at length (see this book's appendix for my interview questions). Participants spoke mostly and extensively about their pasts, their activism, and their tensions and resolutions. I make this statement not as a strike at participants; I know all of them to be good academics and administrators who at the very least keep up with writing center and rhetoric and composition scholarship, while a number of them publish, present, and generate knowledge in these areas. Instead, I bring it up to shed light on my colleague's in-jest observation about writing center labor and life. Activism is a major framework that impacts the writing center discipline's conferences, call for papers and proposals, and a thread of its current research. Yet who is doing this work? Often, it is women, queer people, people of color, and all intersections thereof. Lerner (2019) suggests that, despite agreeing with the researchers' claims, he doesn't know what to do about the tumultuous labor conditions examined in *The Working Lives of New Writing Center Directors* (2016) and other such texts, articulating that other such texts fail to account for identity work and labor conditions (Lerner 2019, 463). I further suggest that I don't know how to make sense of the phenomenon in which we fail to consider the bodies the doing the work most often. If particular labors fall upon queer people and people of color with more regularity, as cited throughout this book, I don't why or how to continue working as if such an imbalance of labor does not exist. The push for activism in writing centers is a necessary nudge, one that suggests, as most of us believe, that writing centers are dynamic sites where much happens—tutoring certainly but also many other intersectional and identity-based exchanges and possibilities. An attention, however, to who is drawn to, tasked with, and pressured to do this labor, however well-intentioned, through local and disciplinary nudges is critical.

LEARNING FROM QUEER TENSION

A distinct reality is that our queer colleagues are bullied and mobbed at their universities regularly in both implicit and explicit ways. Beyond that, they are erased from the discipline and impacted by national and global landscapes that pose difficulties for and enact violence against queer people. Current scholarship that acts as the tensions chapter's primary framework (Elder and Davila 2019) claims—rightly, I believe—that higher education institutions are ripe with such interpersonal violence and offer, however problematically, the perfect conditions for it. We only need to pause to reflect upon higher education's current, competitive landscapes, its labor conditions, and its subjective hierarchies, just to name a few dynamics that give way to bullying and mobbing among supposed colleagues. The point is this violence happens frequently. And it happens beyond what is unspoken and what participant James names as the tensions he "can't put his finger on." Every side whisper and implicit transphobic implication is a direct assault on participants. The word *fag* is present in this book more times than I can count. A nervous laughter accompanies one lesbian participant's recollection of her boss's response when the participant came out to her: "I couldn't fire you if I wanted to." And these occurrences don't happen where we think they do, should, or ought to, because of our assumptions about regional politics. In fact, queer East Coast participants disclosed explicit and implicit name-calling as often, if not slightly more frequently, than those from the South and the Midwest.

Participant perspectives leaned toward discussing local occurrences, meaning they tended to narrate things that happened at their home institutions. This project did not often delve into disciplinary bullying that takes place implicitly and explicitly, when, for example, queer, raced, or intersectional scholarship is rejected, forgotten, or uncited (Brian does direct us to these realities of publishing erasure, while Mike does speak about relationships among bullying and scholarly production). And surprisingly, participants did not delve into queer or raced scholarship rejected in double-blind review or bring up scenarios in which an editor suggests scholarship be revised in order to include non-queer and white scholars and scholarship mostly irrelevant to queer and raced work. All are forms of implicit bullying at least, and all are forms of labor for queer writing center scholars navigating a discipline.

Returning the chapter 4's claims about research rarely surfacing as a conversation point with participants, participants' activisms and tensions traced in this book have complicated their relationships to disciplinary productivity and research. On one hand, activism is sometimes published about, giving way to fresh and energizing projects that propel forward the writing center discipline. Returning to my colleague's in-jest comment in the previous section, perhaps there is truth to the tongue-in-cheek criticism of the role of and fixation on activism in writing centers. Is there perhaps a way to better do, write about, and materialize it in ways that help practitioners of this project and of the field who ultimately may be most vulnerable, namely queer writing center scholars like these participants? Finding balance among activism, production, and a sustainable discipline with productive scholars (with, I'll say it, more queer research foci) is of utmost importance.

LIMITATIONS

This book's claims rely on perspectives from twenty queer writing center practitioners, which is both an asset and drawback. On one hand, the participant pool was rich and diverse for the writing center field, which is not diverse; on the other hand, the recruitment methods relied on the assumption that queer directors were, first and foremost, out, out at work, and willing to talk about their outness and their work—which is not a set of assumptions nor a framework that works for or is safe for everyone. To even agree to participate, people would have to have some comfort and sense of safety about being out. These assumptions, without a doubt, impacted the data, but what the researcher brings to the table impacts any empirical research project. With this said, I as a researcher do wonder what stories remain to be told because a research-based interview, by and large, inhibits their telling. For example, what stories about bullying remain untold because of fear of being outed, punished, or worse at home institutions? And what subversive activisms exist beyond what participants shared here because of concerns about safety? What perspectives may be left out due to a lack of white, institutional, or disciplinary privilege? Many of these questions surface for me, which is to say that the study, like any empirical investigation that seeks to make meaning about a phenomenon involving people, has limitations. While I argue that the study and the methods are sound, the project does rest on several assumptions. For one thing, studying writing center work and queer identity is, in and of itself, going to present limitations. But as a vested, committed, and queer researcher myself, I did make concerted efforts to mitigate limitations in order to develop and complete a study that is valid and meaningful. I sought the support of queer and nonqueer writing center scholars, both senior and midcareer, about this study's framework and its drafts. I also attended the 2016 International Writing Centers Association Summer Institute. There, I received feedback from leaders and fellow attendees, some of whom are queer, about the study itself, its design, its methods, and its instruments, as well as my application for conducting human research at my previous university.

This book's methods could be replicated. Another scholar could conduct a similar study to contribute to this area of study and critique mine. A project like this is, however, is an instance in which the field's current reliance and fixation on replicable, aggregable, and data-driven methods is both an asset and a burden. A replication crisis certainly pervades disciplines that rely on scientific methods and generalizability, but perhaps English, rhetoric and composition, and writing center studies are not experiencing such a dearth, and perhaps a replication crisis would impact our world with less intensity, given the lessened stakes of our work (i.e., however, important the work of writing centers, we're not curing cancer, for example). So, a focus on replicating my study would be fantastic, as I would love to know how other queer, transgender, and of color researchers and participants would interface with such a project. That said, I don't know that I want a researcher to fixate on replicating this study and its methods, given that I think the writing center world just needs more queer, transgender, and of color empirical research in general. So do it, do more of it, and don't worry about replicating this study. Let's seek to get more empirically focused, voice-based writing center projects out there, period. In this vein, as I stated in the methods section of my introduction, I do however think a queer body is necessary in that not just anyone—a straight person, for example—ought to take up this project for replication. My queer body in the space and in the establishment of participant trust is not "replicable." Such embodied phenomena of execution and trust aren't present in current writing center RAD research.

The writing center discipline is already a small field and notably undiverse. We have research to corroborate this claim (Valles, Babcock, and

Jackson 2017), as we are mostly made up of straight white women. Thus, a study about queer people in the writing center field talking about their work will draw from an already-small participant pool. As stated above, such a study assumes people are out and willing to talk about their work, and that their positions are stable enough to desire participation. At the end of each interview, when asked about the desire for anonymity, participants were comfortable being named in the project using their actual first and last names—all twenty of them. I chose to give pseudonyms for reasons outlined in the book's methods section, but I was struck by this participant perspective. Despite a relatively diverse pool across gender, race, institution type, and position type, it was quite telling about each participant's relationship to their directorship and their comfort, freedom, bravery, and orientation to their work and sites.

Most participants are white and cisgender. In fact, most identify as gay men or lesbians, despite my use of the word *queer* for brevity and readability throughout the book. Just one participant is transgender, while others identify as nonbinary or gender noncomforming, with one other identifying as a "boyish"-presenting lesbian. No participant identified explicitly as bisexual or asexual, and only one identified as pansexual. While this is a diverse pool for the writing center world, certainly it is perhaps not as diverse in terms of queer communities. With this said, I often have reservations about pairing the lives of white gay men and lesbians with those of other subject positions simply because of white, cisgender, race, and often class privilege. A gay, white, employed, upper-middle-class man or woman arguably lives a fairly seamless life, although occasionally trying and traumatic, when compared, for example, to a transgender woman of color with a working-class background. Certainly, these kinds of comparisons impact any "community," but as a gay white man, I have long had reservations about gay and lesbian identities being pooled together with and dominating the LGBTQA initialism. Queer, Gay, and Lesbian issues are often quite different from transgender issues. I am, of course, happy to showcase transgender, gender noncomforming, and pansexual identities in this project, but I will always have personal reservations about doing them justice and implying, even by rhetorical and semantic proximity, that they are as privileged as white gay men and white lesbians of middle- to upper-middle-class standing. In doing this work, I rely on G Patterson's (2019) rhetorical guidance, which I unpacked in this book's introduction, alongside Pritchard's (2019) calls to be accountable to and inclusive of transgender scholars and scholars of color when working with and writing about them.

For reasons alluded to above, snowball sampling was tricky. I asked participants to suggest peers and colleagues they thought might want to participate and in most all cases, this process worked out beautifully. Only once did it fail when a participant suggested another prospective participant who, when I reached out for recruitment, disclosed politely that she was not in fact a lesbian. Snowball sampling's only other limitation was, perhaps, that it often pointed back to just how undiverse the writing center field is, almost by default. White people snowballed white people. It was the IWCA LGBTQA special interest groups that in actuality diversified the project in that I was able to recruit a second Black participant and a transgender participant, neither of whom could think of another Black or transgender person for recruitment. I say that with no criticism of those participants but as yet another example that shows our field is just very white and very cisgender. And even when we're gay or lesbian, we're likely inhabiting cisgender bodies and are often squarely middle class. These realities impact not only studies and research but also just the state of the writing center field. I did also often wonder whom I was missing despite my best of intentions to distribute the call in as many places as I could, which I thought would attract a diverse pool of participants. Snowball sampling from a core of five very out and established queer writing center scholars, and recruitment at international conferences, SIGs, and the LGBTQA SIG listserv still samples from privileged people and places, which is to say there are likely queer writing center people out there I just did not reach. Yet my sample size of twenty is fairly notable compared to award-winning writing center research that traces labor, as Caswell, Grutsch McKinney, and Jackson (2016) and Geller and Denny (2013) do—two projects that showcase the labor of nine and thirteen participants, respectively.

PARTING WORDS

Implications for Writing Center Administration

A queerer approach to writing center work, as described by queer directors, has much to offer the writing center field. I've said before, especially to my nonqueer audiences, that I don't think queer writing center directors are just so darn special, nor do I think nonqueer directors are clueless with no sense of a formed identity around their writing center work. What still strikes me, however, is something I noticed the first time I read the conclusion of *The Working Lives of New Writing Center Directors.* Participants spoke about all sorts of labor and labored dynamics in their first years on the job but said nothing about their identities. Like this one, the study was quite white, certainly. But even so, even as the researchers note (Caswell, Grutsch McKinney, and Jackson 2016, 180), participants just did not "go there"—didn't delve into gender, sexuality, race, class, ability, or the like. For me, omissions strongly suggest that, despite work like Denny's (2011; 2019) and Doucette's (2011) we, as a collective discipline, do not see queer identity as wrapped up in, applicable to, and affording answers and perspectives critical for our administrative work. This book is one step in a direction for change, with the intent to inspire more research. At face value, writing centers are where writing and writing support take place in university settings. We have a disciplinary history that makes claims to, corroborates, and contests what writing centers are, how they function, how they serve writers, and how they are led. The labor of site leadership is paramount in writing center work. As practitioners, we know a leader can make or break the site and its mission, vision, and outcomes. As a queer person focused on justice and equity in all my professional endeavors, I write this book with attention to how these frameworks blend to generate knowledge about administration, queerness, and work. In this sense, this book attempts to showcase and celebrate yet offers an occasional yet loud and sobering glimpse at the labor itself. And how we do or don't talk about it yet.

I hope the book signals what's possible in writing center administration for queer and nonqueer audiences. And I hope I have offered the writing center world more frameworks for understanding our labor at a time when such conversations are critical. Writing centers close, they are relocated, and they are paired with sister and not-so-sister departments while universities shift and change, rarely for the better. While a writing center that closes is no one's wish, I am not of the mindset that moves or changes are always bad. What I would call "bad," however, is when we don't know ourselves in our directorships and we don't know how to harness experience (or capital, as this book would have it) for our empowerment. Writing centers are evolving alongside a new generation of students, expectations, and higher education landscapes. In just one glimpse into the twenty-first-century writing center, Denny, Nordlof, and Salem (2018) explain that, as first-generation and working-class students (often of color) enter university at unprecedented rates, these students' rightful expectations misalign with our oft-entrenched methods and practices. Alongside these generational, cultural, and educational shifts in which stakeholders fall out of touch, naming and talking about modern work is a critical first step. Yet we must also complicate and contextualize this labor alongside our lived conditions as writing center directors. In this sense, queer people may have much to teach nonqueer directors about understanding writing center work and drawing from all our own queer experiences that might afford us enriched methods for, say, linking our pasts to our administrative presents. Or doing responsible, self-care-focused writing center activism regardless of our backgrounds while also not burning out, publishing to advance the discipline and ourselves, and not becoming workhorses based on what our identities might afford our centers and universities. Or interfacing productively with institutions, colleagues, or situations that are just plain tense and ripe with professional consequence, which despite fabulous recent scholarship in rhetoric and composition, writing centers, and the like, is still an underexamined research area, notwithstanding a quite pressing need to better understand such dynamics.

This book regularly points to labor imbalances among queer and raced bodies in administrative positions. Queer people, people of color, and people whose marginalized identities intersect are doing different work than nonmarginalized colleagues. Sometimes, in fact, they are doing more work than nonmarginalized colleagues. Imagine doing the vast duties of a writing center director, then having a queer student drop in, close the door, and confess suicidal ideation. Imagine that in the same position you are also called a homophobic or transphobic slur. Now imagine these how these phenomena would impact your labor, especially your tangible, countable productivity, whether publishing or presenting or seeking grants for your writing center. If nothing else, I believe these labored realities call for nonqueer audiences, as the tensions chapter examines, to consider Green's (2018) call for accompliceship: she asks white and privileged scholars to abandon alliance in favor of accomplicing, wherein "word and deed" (29) hold more rhetorical and material weight for supporting and advocating for colleagues of color. When accompliceship is operationalized for queer people, nonqueer colleagues can listen to and for these distinctions—these imbalances—in order to be accomplices in the writing center world. The field depends on it, in fact, in terms of research, diversity, and sustainability: research in terms of encouraging projects like this one but also understanding how the labor imbalances described in this book may stifle research because queer people have difficulty getting it done; diversity in that things don't happen when queer people aren't in the room (as participant Brian reminds us about race in writing centers), thus recruitment and retention of queer people is paramount; and sustainability as framed in the aforementioned statement, which echoes Lerner's (2019) claim that it's difficult to address writing center labor realities without understanding identities, people, and conditions of and for that labor.

To use this book's key framework for a few more parting words to writing center colleagues, if we can continue to see the capital each of us, queer and nonqueer, holds that makes us ready for and effective in our work, we'll continue to advance as a discipline in our research and our practice. We might not always like what we find nor the realities of what happens when we do our work (think: the downsides of writing center activism, or the tensions and bullying we all experience), but complicating how we talk about writing center labor (in this case, through a queer lens) is critical to our work. The stories of queer writing center workers may be one starting ticket.

Implications for Writing Program Administration and Writing-across-the-Curriculum Administration

WPA and WAC administrators may look at this book as uniquely, if not narrowly, central to writing centers. Writing center administrative labor is certainly its own kind of work, distinct and often disparate from WPA and WAC work, despite partnerships that span one or more such entities. At present, I am a faculty WAC director and have performed writing center director and WPA duties at previous institutions, hence the reasons I know these writing studies administrative positions are distinct. Alexander and Wallace (2009), in their examination of queer studies and rhetoric and composition, argue that a "queer turn" in the field was not only necessary but critical and omnipresent for the discipline (184). Queer scholars as of late (Kopelson 2013; Banks, Cox, and Dadas 2019) have since questioned whether such a "turn," despite its dire necessity and rich possibility, ever happened. This question could certainly apply to current conversations about WPA and WAC administrative worlds. The recent text *WPAs in Transition: Navigating Educational Leadership Positions* (Wooten et al. 2018), for example, while a critical, necessary investigation into how WPAs move in, out of, and within their positions across time and space, seems to miss opportunities for contributors to theorize queerness and queer bodies within such mobilities. As I read, I kept wondering about how queer administrative narratives theorized alongside mobility might make an already-strong collection even stronger. I mention this research because the text is strong, but as a queer administrator myself gifted with this book's participants perspectives, I identify with the skepticism that recent WPA and rhetoric and composition scholars have of Alexander and Wallace's (2009) "queer turn" claim. Given the critical partnerships among writing center, WPA, and WAC sites, I am left wondering what a queer, person-based glimpse into queer WPA work would look like empirically, reflecting back to this book's participant narratives. And while the WPA research world has aptly and soundly traced relationships among queerness, queers, bodies, and administration (see this book's literature review), WAC administration and WAC work in general still are quite unexamined through queer lenses.

Implications for Higher Education Administration

Higher education studies often focus on curricula, pedagogy, and student affairs but rarely examine what happens when bodies inhabit administrative spaces. This book's participant perspectives afford higher education administration much in the way of tracing and theorizing about queer bodies in academic leadership roles. I argue that the promise and possibility of queer bodies in such spaces can impact the collective, big-picture nature of our work. I reflect on my work as queer writing center director at my past institution. There, queer people, people of color, and people with intersecting marginalized identities often held early to midcareer staff positions, despite the university being a Hispanic-serving institution with a dire need to support its Hispanic and Latinx students and recruit, retain, and support its few Black students. All the while, its queer outreach, support, and programming ebbed and flowed, often dependent on student-driven initiatives rather than grounded in and paired with a university-wide efforts among faculty, staff, and students to craft such spaces. Further, rarely did these intersectionally diverse bodies inhabit roles in upper administrative leadership. Change surfaced when our university selected a woman of color to be its president, the first in its history following five white male presidents. In many ways, the university's energy changed, with new life made possible with a woman of color as university president, who in many ways, better reflected the student body and who offered an embodied, administrative lesson about what's possible when attention is paid to diverse bodies in university leadership. The same is true for this book. I do not claim all writing centers directors ought to be queer, or Black, or transgender, nor any subjectivity framed in this book. But I do think studies like this teach us about what's different and what's possible when diverse (for these purposes, read queer) leaders lead in our institutions of higher education.

Directions for the Writing Center World

I close this book with inspiration from Jessica Restaino's (2012) *First Semester: Graduate Students, Teaching Writing, and the Challenge of the*

Middle Ground. Restaino's conclusion offers a beautiful discussion of how researchers might build meaning about the teaching and research of writing from the lived experiences of graduate teaching assistants, reframing the epistemological tenets of the teaching of writing through this underexamined demographic. In her closing thoughts, she reminds readers that in order to avoid "potential misuse of theory as dislocated from diverse contexts," she has not "described a model program or offered a set of best practices" (106). While Restaino's book traces the lived experiences of a demographic distinct from this book's participants, I can't help but draw connections to her empirical study, her analyses, and her closing thoughts. Like this study does, Restaino (2012) worked with an underexamined group, sought to challenge common knowledge about rhetoric and composition research and practice, and offered not just one vision for her research but many (106). I hope to do the same.

Ultimately, I hope this book, from participants' and my words, can contribute to and perhaps challenge what we talk about when we talk about writing center labor. Yet, I do not think there are easy answers, nor is there one administrative vision for what these queer perspectives afford writing center labor studies. Throughout this book, I have used the word *unicorn* on several occasions to describe participant work. I end this book with further insight into this descriptor. During my first interview for this project, I spoke for well over an hour with Mike. What is not obvious from this book is that interviews were more like conversations with friends. I asked questions, which led to lots of chatting. In talking through the paradox of queer writing center leadership—it's gratifying yet laborious, if not tense, work—Mike and I paused following an interview question. In the transcript, I said, "It's like [queer writing center directors] are unicorns," but we said the word "unicorns" in unison. I only hope you will listen to and hear these perspectives and find inspiration in them. Despite the fact that I frame this queer unicorn theme as a paradox of this book, I do believe we should err on the side of perceiving "unicorndom" as a concept that affords the field something special. These directors can teach us about what's possible in our writing center work, whether working with tutors, working as site leaders, or working to help queer and nonqueer people alike with living, thriving, and surviving in a post-*Pulse* world.

APPENDIX

INTERVIEW QUESTIONS

LGBTQ people often have a story related to their coming-out process. If you're comfortable doing so, would you share an abbreviated version of that story?

How did you come to have a professional life in a writing center?

How do those two aspects of your identity complement or conflict with each other?

Tell me about a time when being LGBTQ has impacted your experience in your writing center, or when a writing center experience impacted your experience as an LGBTQ person.

Describe a moment where you felt tension or conflict around being WC director and LGBTQ?

Describe a moment where you felt at ease or resolved around being WC director and LGBTQ?

How might your LGBTQ identity impact your conscious, administrative choices (about philosophies, practices, pedagogies, and theories) in your writing center?

Do you have anything you would like to add to your interview today or that others I might speak with?

DOI: 10.7330/9781646421497.c006

NOTES

CHAPTER 1: INTRODUCTION

1. I use *queer* in this book instead of *lesbian, gay, bisexual, transgender, queer,* and *asexual* (LGBTQA) simply for the sake of readability. I say more about this decision in this chapter's "About This Book" section.
2. I use the words *director, administrator, practitioner,* and *professional* rather interchangeably in this book to describe people who officially lead writing centers. I realize the field has taken up this distinction (Caswell, Grutsch McKinney, and Jackson, 2016; Geller and Denny, 2013) and encourages scholars to be mindful, intentional, and inclusive when referring to our writing center work, as I have done my best to be. I reiterate this point in this chapter's "About This Book" section.
3. I coauthored a book chapter about my staff's request that I respond to the *Pulse* events. I discuss the chapter at length in chapter 3.
4. Many writing centers administrators work long hours, often staffing centers and leading tutors into evening hours, hence the phrase *night job.*
5. My interview questions are included in this book's appendix.
6. I am on the fence about lore's place in writing center scholarship, as readers might notice from my inclination to value lore but also seek empirical investigations into queer writing center work, as this book seeks to do.

CHAPTER 3: QUEER WRITING CENTER LABOR AND/AS ACTIVISM

1. PrEP stands for preexposure prophylaxis, or a daily medicine taken by HIV-negative people at high risk for seroconversion to prevent HIV infection (HIV.gov).

CHAPTER 4: QUEER WRITING CENTER LABOR AND/AS TENSION

1. Here, I avoid the term *microaggression.* I feel that the word is limiting, too bound up in popular culture, and I do not wish to evoke that particular sentiment.

REFERENCES

AIDS Coalition To Unleash Power (ACT-UP). Last accessed September 25, 2019. https://actupny.org/.

Alexander, Jonathan. 2008. *Literacy, Sexuality, Pedagogy: Theory and Practice for Composition Studies.* Logan: Utah State University Press.

Alexander, Jonathan. 2009. "Literacy and Diversity: A Provocation." *WPA: Writing Program Administration* 33 (1–2): 164–71.

Alexander, Jonathan, and David Wallace. 2009. "The Queer Turn in Composition Studies: Reviewing and Assessing an Emerging Scholarship." *College Composition and Communication* 61 (1): 300–320.

Alexander, Jonathan, and William P. Banks. 2009. "Queer Eye for the Comp Program: Towards a Queer Critique of WPA Work." In *The Writing Program Interrupted: Making Space for Critical Discourse*, edited by Donna G. Strickland and Jeanne Gunner, 86–98. Portsmouth: Boynton/Cook.

Balester, Valerie M., and James McDonald. 2001. "A View of Status and Working Conditions: Relations between Writing Program and Writing Center Directors." *WPA: Writing Program Administration* 24 (3): 59–82.

Banks, William P. 2012. "Queer Outcomes: Hacking the Source Code for the WPA Outcomes Statement for First-Year Composition." *WPA: Writing Program Administration* 36 (1): 204–208.

Banks, William P., Matthew B. Cox, and Caroline Dadas, eds. 2019. *Re/Orienting Writing Studies: Queer Methods/Queer Projects.* Logan: Utah State University Press.

Blakemore, Erin. 2018. "Gay Conversion Therapy's Disturbing Eighteenth-Century Origins." *History*, June 22, 2018. Last modified June 28, 2019. https://www.history.com/news/gay-conversion-therapy-origins-19th-century.

Boquet, Elizabeth H. 2002. *Noise from the Center.* Logan: Utah State University Press.

Bousquet, Mark. 2008. *How the University Works: Higher Education and the Low-Wage Nation.* New York: New York University Press.

Bourdieu, Pierre. 1986. "The Forms of Capital." In *Handbook of Theory and Research for the Sociology of Education*, edited by John G. Richardson, 241–58. New York: Greenwood.

Bratta, Phil, and Malea Powell. 2016. "Introduction to the Special Issue: Entering the Cultural Rhetorics Conversations." *Enculturation: A Journal of Rhetoric, Writing and Culture* 21. Accessed July 3, 2019. http://enculturation.net/entering-the-cultural-rhetorics-conversations.

Brooks-Gillies, Marilee. 2018. "Constellations Across Cultural Rhetorics and Writing Centers." *The Peer Review: A Journal for Writing Center Practitioners* 2 (Special Issue). Last accessed August 2, 2019. http://thepeerreview-iwca.org/issues/relationality-si/constellations-across-cultural-rhetorics-and-writing-centers/.

Brooks-Gillies, Marilee, Nicole Emmelhainz, Deirdre Garriott, and Scott Whiddon. "When Institutional and Disciplinary Cultures Clash: The Challenges of Supporting Social Justice As Pre-Tenure and Non-Tenure-Track Writing Center Administrators." Presentation given at the Annual Meeting of the International Writing Centers Association, Atlanta, GA, 2018.

DOI: 10.7330/9781646421497.c007

Brown, Sarah. "Nearly Half of Undergraduates Are Students of Color. But Black Students Lag Behind." *The Chronicle of Higher Education*, February 14, 2019. https://www.chronicle.com/article/Nearly-Half-of-Undergraduates/245692

Carter, Chris. 2008. *Rhetoric and Resistance in the Corporate Academy*. New York: Hampton Press.

Caswell, Nicole I., Jackie Grutsch McKinney, and Rebecca Jackson. 2016. *The Working Lives of New Writing Center Directors*. Logan: Utah State University Press.

Centers for Disease Control. 2019a. "HIV and African American Gay and Bisexual Men." Last modified September 6. https://www.cdc.gov/hiv/group/msm/bmsm.html.

Centers for Disease Control. 2019b. "HIV and Gay and Bisexual Men." Last modified September 9. https://www.cdc.gov/hiv/group/msm/index.html.

Condon, Frankie, and Bobbi Olsen. 2016. "Building a House for Linguistic Diversity: Writing Centers, English-Language Teaching and Learning, and Social Justice." In *Tutoring Second Language Writers*, edited by Shanti Bruce and Ben Rafoth, 27–52. Logan: Utah State University Press.

Cox, Matthew B. 2019. "Working Closets: Mapping Queer Professional Discourses and Why Professional Communication Studies Needs Queer Rhetorics." *Journal of Business and Technical Communication* 33 (1): 1–25.

Crain, Marion, Winifred Poster, and Miriam Cherry. 2016. Introduction to *Invisible labor: Hidden Work in the Contemporary World*, 3–27. Edited by Marion Crain, Winifred Poster, and Miriam Cherry. Berkeley: University of California P.

Crenshaw, Kimberly Williams. 1991. "Mapping the Margins: Intersectionality, Identity Politics, and Violence Against Women of Color." *Stanford Law Review* 43 (6): 1241–99.

Crenshaw, Kimberly Williams. 2018. *On Intersectionality: Essential Writings*. New York: New Press.

Crisp, Sally. 2000. "On Leading the Writing Center: A Sort of Credo and Some Advice for Beginners and Oldtimers, Too." *Writing Lab Newsletter* 24 (6): 1–5.

Dadas, Caroline. 2013. "Reaching the Professional: The Locations of the Rhetoric and Composition Job Market." *College Composition and Communication* 65 (1): 67–89.

Dadas, Caroline. 2018. "Interview Practices as Accessibility: The Academic Job Market." *Composition Forum* 39. Accessed June 25, 2019. https://compositionforum.com/issue/39/interview-practices.php.

Daniel, James. 2020. "Burning Out: Writing and The Self in the Era of Terminal Productivity." *Enculturation: A Journal of Rhetoric, Writing, and Culture* 30. Last accessed June 15, 2020: http://enculturation.net/Burning_Out.

Daniels, Arlene Kaplan. 1987. "Invisible Work." *Social Problems* 35 (5): 403–15.

Degner, Hillary, Kylie Wojciehowski, and Christopher Giroux. 2015. "Opening Closed Doors: A Rationale for Creating a Safe Space for Tutors with Mental Health Concerns or Illness." *Praxis: A Writing Center Journal* 13 (1): 27–37.

Denny, Harry C. 2005. "Queering the Writing Center." *Writing Center Journal* 25 (2): 39–62.

Denny, Harry C. 2010. "A Curious Silence and a Long-ish Response," WCenter Listserv, October 8, 2010. http://lyris.ttu.edu/read/messages?id=14800124#14800124

Denny, Harry C. 2011. *Facing the Center: Toward an Identity Politics of One-to-One Mentoring*. Logan: Utah State University Press.

Denny, Harry C. 2013. "Queer Eye for the WPA." *WPA: Writing Program Administration* 37 (1): 186–98.

Denny, Harry C. 2014. "Of Sticks and Stones, Words That Wounds, and Actions Speaking Louder: When Academic Bullying Becomes Everyday Oppression." *Workplace: A Journal for Academic Labor* 24: 1–8.

Denny, Harry C., John Nordlof, and Lori Salem. 2018. " 'Tell Me Exactly What It Was That I Was Doing That Was So Bad': Understanding the Needs and Expectations of Working-Class Students in Writing Centers." *Writing Center Journal* 37 (1): 67–100.

Denny, Harry C., Robert Mundy, Liliana M. Naydan, Richard Severe, and Anna Sicari, eds. 2019. *Out in the Center: Public Controversies and Private Struggles.* Logan: Utah State University Press.

Diab, Rasha, Thomas Ferrel, Beth Godbee, and Neil Simkins. 2012. "A Multi-Dimensional Pedagogy for Racial Justice in Writing Centers." *Praxis: A Writing Center Journal* 10 (1): 1–8. Last accessed July 15, 2019. http://www.praxisuwc.com/diab-godbee-ferrell-simpkins-101.

Dixon, Elise. 2017. "Uncomfortably Queer: Everyday Moments in the Writing Center." *The Peer Review: A Journal for Writing Center Practitioners* 1(2). Last accessed August 2, 2019. http://thepeerreview-iwca.org/issues/braver-spaces/uncomfortably-queer-everyday-moments-in-the-writing-center/.

Doucette, Jonathan. 2011. "Composing Queers: The Subversive Potential of the Writing Center." *Young Scholars in Writing* 8: 5–15.

Driscoll, Dana Lynn, and Sherry Wynn Perdue. 2012. "Theory, Lore, and More: An Analysis of RAD Research in *The Writing Center Journal*, 1980–2009." *Writing Center Journal* 32 (2): 11–39.

Ehrenreich, Barbara. 2001. *Nickel and Dimed: On (Not) Getting By in America.* New York: Holt.

Ehrenreich, Barbara. 2005. *Bait and Switch: The (Futile) Pursuit of the American Dream.* New York: Holt.

Elder, Cristyn, and Bethany Davila, editors. 2019. *Defining, Locating, and Addressing Bullying in the WPA Workplace.* Logan: Utah State University Press.

Elliott, M. A. 1990. "Writing Center Directors: Why Faculty Status Fits." *Writing Lab Newsletter* 14 (7): 1–4.

Eliot, Mary. 1996. "Coming Out in the Classroom: A Return to the Hard Place." *College English* 58: 693–708.

Eodice, Michele. 2010. "Introduction to Queering the Writing Center." *Writing Center Journal* 30 (1), *An Alternative History*: 92–94.

Extravaganza, Venus. 1990. *Paris Is Burning.* By Jennie Livingston. Off-White Productions.

Faison, Wonderful. 2019. "Writing as a Practice of Freedom: HCBU Writing Centers as Sites of Liberatory Freedom." *Praxis: A Writing Center Journal* 16 (2): 58–59.

Faison, Wonderful, and Anna Trevino. 2017. "Race, Retention, Language, and Literacy: The Hidden Curriculum of the Writing Center." *The Peer Review: A Journal for Writing Center Practitioners* 1(2). Last accessed July 31, 2019. http://thepeerreview-iwca.org/issues/braver-spaces/race-retention-language-and-literacy-the-hidden-curriculum-of-the-writing-center/.

Faison, Wonderful, Talisha Haltiwanger Morrison, Katie Levin, Elijah Simmons, Jasmine Kar Tang, and Keli Tucker. 2019. "Potential for and Barriers to Actionable Anti-Racism in the Writing Center: Views from the IWCA Special Interest Group on Antiracism Activism." *Praxis: A Writing Center Journal* 16 (2). Last accessed September 25, 2019. http://www.praxisuwc.com/162-faison-et-al.

Fels, Dawn, Clint Gardner, Maggie Herb, and Liliana Naydan. 2016. "Toward an Investigation into the Working Conditions of Non-Tenure Line, Contingent Writing Center Works." *Forum: Issues about Part-Time and Contingent Faculty* 20 (1): A10–A16.

Garcia, Romeo. 2017. "Unmaking Gringo Centers." *Writing Center Journal* 36 (1): 29–60.

Geller, Anne Ellen, Frankie Condon, and Meg Carroll. 2011. "Bold: The Everyday Writing Center and the Production of New Knowledge in Anti-Racist Theory and Practice." In *Writing Centers and the New Racism: A Call for Sustainable Dialogue and Change,* edited by Laura Greenfield and Karen Rowan, 101–23. Logan: Utah State University Press.

Geller, Anne Ellen, and Harry C. Denny. 2013. "Of Ladybugs, Low Status, and Loving the Job: Writing Center Professionals Navigating Their Careers" *Writing Center Journal* 33 (1): 96–129.

Geller, Anne Ellen, Michele Eodice, Frankie Condon, Meg Carroll, and Elizabeth H. Boquet. 2007. *The Everyday Writing Center: A Community of Practice*. Logan: Utah State University Press.

Goins, Elizabeth, and Frederick Coyle Heard. 2012. "Diversity in the Writing Center." *Praxis: A Writing Center Journal* 10 (2). Last accessed September 25, 2019. http://www.praxisuwc.com/from-the-editors-101.

Goodblar, David. "4 Ideas for Avoiding Faculty Burnout." *The Chronicle of Higher Education*, April 23, 2018. https://www.chronicle.com/article/4-Ideas-for-Avoiding-Faculty/243010.

Green, Neisha-Anne S. 2018. "Moving Beyond Alright: And the Emotional Toll of This, My Life Matters Too, in the Writing Center Work." *Writing Center Journal* 37 (1): 15–34.

Greenfield, Laura. 2019. *Radical Writing Center Praxis: A Paradigm for Ethical Political Engagement*. Logan: Utah State University Press.

Greenfield, Laura, and Karen Rowan, eds. 2011. *Writing Centers and the New Racism: A Call for Sustainable Dialogue and Change*. Logan: Utah State University Press.

Grimm, Nancy Maloney. 1999. *Good Intentions: Writing Center Work for Postmodern Times*. Portsmouth, NH: Boynton/Cook-Heinneman.

Hall, R. Mark. 2010. "A Social Capital View of Writing Center-WAC Partnership." *Praxis: A Writing Center Journal* 7 (2). Last accessed March 19, 2020. http://www.praxisuwc.com/hall-72.

Hall, R. Mark. 2017. *Around the Texts of Writing Center Work: An Inquiry-Based Approach to Tutor Education*. Logan: Utah State University Press.

Hallman Martini, Rebecca. 2018. "Empirical and Sociopolitical Intersections in Writing Center Research." Paper presented at the Annual Convention of the International Writing Centers Association, Atlanta, GA.

Hallman Martini, Rebecca, and Travis Webster. 2017a. "What Online Spaces Afford Us in the Age of Campus Carry, 'Wall-Building,' and Orlando's Pulse Tragedy." In *Handbook of Research on Writing and Composing in the Age of MOOCs*, eds. Liz Monske and Kris Blair, 278–293. Hershey: IGI Global.

Hallman Martini, Rebecca, and Travis Webster. 2017b. "Writing Centers as Brave/r Spaces: A Special Issue Introduction." *The Peer Review: A Journal for Writing Center Practitioners* 1(2). Last accessed July 31, 2019. http://thepeerreview-iwca.org/issues/braver-spaces/writing-centers-as-braver-spaces-a-special-issue-introduction/.

Healy, Dave. 1995. "Writing Center Directors: An Emerging Portrait of the Profession." *WPA: Writing Program Administration* 18 (3): 26–43.

Hermann, Jacob. 2017. "Brave/r Spaces Versus Safer Spaces for LGBTQ+ in the Writing Center: Theory and Practice at the University of Kansas." *The Peer Review: A Journal for Writing Center Practitioners* 1(2). Last accessed July 31, 2019. http://thepeerreview-iwca.org/issues/braver-spaces/braver-spaces-vs-safe-spaces-for-lgbtq-in-the-writing-center-theory-and-practice-at-the-university-of-kansas/.

HIV.Gov. "Pre-Exposure Prophylaxis." Last updated June 26, 2019. https://www.hiv.gov/hiv-basics/hiv-prevention/using-hiv-medication-to-reduce-risk/pre-exposure-prophylaxis.

Hochschild, Arlie Russell. 1979. *The Managed Heart: Commercialization of Human Feeling*. Berkeley: University of California Press.

Human Rights Campaign. 2019. "Violence Against the Transgender Community in 2019." Last modified 2019. https://www.hrc.org/resources/violence-against-the-transgender-community-in-2019.

Ianetta, Melissa, Linda Bergmann, Lauren Fitzgerald, Carol Peterson Haviland, Lisa Lebduska, and Mary Wislocki. 2006. "Polylog: Are Writing Center Directors Writing Program Administrators?" *Composition Studies* 34 (2): 11–42.

Inoue, Asao. 2019. "How Do We Language So People Stop Killing Each Other, Or What Do We Do About White Language Supremacy?" Chair's Address presented at the

Annual Convention of the Conference on College Composition and Communication, Pittsburgh, PA.

International Writing Centers Association. 2017. "Position Statements." http://writing centers.org/position-statements/.

International Writing Centers Association. 2018. "IWCA 2018 Atlanta: The Citizen Center." http://writingcenters.org/wp-content/uploads/2018/09/Final-IWCA2018-Program .pdf.

International Writing Centers Association. 2019. "IWCA 2019 Columbus: The Art of It All." http://writingcenters.org/annual-conference-2/.

Isaacs, Emily, and Melinda Knight. 2014. "A Bird's Eye View of Writing Center Directors: Institutional Infrastructure, Scope and Programmatic Issues, Reported Practices." *WPA: Writing Program Administration* 37 (2): 36–67.

Kahn, Seth, William B. Lalicker, and Amy Lynch-Biniek, editors. 2019. *Contingency, Exploitation, and Solidarity: Labor and Action in English Composition.* Boulder, CO: University Press of Colorado /The WAC Clearinghouse.

Katz, Jonathan Ned. 1995. *The Invention of Heterosexuality.* Chicago: University of Chicago Press.

Kopelson, Karen. 2013. "Queering the Writing Program: Why Now? How? And Other Contentious Questions." *WPA: Writing Program Administration* 37 (1): 199–213.

LaFrance, Michelle. 2018. "Re: Rubrics to Assess Writing Assignments," wpa-l, October 22, 2018. https://lists.asu.edu/cgi-bin/wa?A2=ind1810&L=wpa-l&F=&S=&P=265269.

LaFrance, Michelle. 2019. *Institutional Ethnography: A Theory and Practice for Writing Studies Researchers.* Logan: Utah State University Press.

LaFrance, Michelle, and Melissa Nicolas. 2012. "Institutional Ethnography as Materialist Framework for Writing Program Research and the Faculty-Staff Standpoints Project." *College Composition and Communication* 64 (1): 130–50.

Lerner, Neal. 2006. "Time Warp: Historical Representations of Writing Center Directors." In *The Writing Center Director's Resource Book,* edited by Christina Murphy and Byron L. Stay, 3–11. New York: Routledge.

Lerner, Neal. 2019. "Growing Pains in the Golden Age: Writing Centers in the Twenty-First Century." *College English* 81 (5): 457–66.

Livingston, Jennie, dir. 1990. *Paris Is Burning.* New York, NY: Off White Productions. Netflix.

Lockett, Alexandria. 2019. "A Touching Place: Womanist Approaches to the Center." In *Out in the Center: Public Controversies and Private Struggles,* edited by Harry Denny, Robert Mundy, Liliana M. Naydan, Richard Severe, and Anna Sicari, 28–42. Logan: Utah State University Press.

Logue, Calvin. 1981. "Transcending Coercion: The Communicative Strategies of Black Slaves on Antebellum Plantations." *Quarterly Journal of Speech* 67: 31–46.

de Mueller, Genevieve Garcia, and Iris Ruiz. 2017. "Race, Silence, and Writing Program Administration: A Qualitative Study of U.S. College Writing Programs." *WPA: Writing Program Administration* 40 (2): 19–39.

McComiskey, Bruce. 2017. *Post-Truth Rhetoric and Composition.* Logan: Utah State University Press.

McKinney, Jackie Grutsch. 2013. *Peripheral Visions for Writing Centers.* Logan: Utah State University Press.

McNamee, Kaidan, and Michelle Miley. 2017. "Writing Center as Homeplace (A Site for Radical Resistance)." *The Peer Review: A Journal for Writing Center Practitioners* 1(2). Last accessed July 31, 2019. http://thepeerreview-iwca.org/issues/braver-spaces/writing -center-as-homeplace-a-site-for-radical-resistance/.

Mackiewicz, Jo, and Isabelle Kramer Thompson. 2018. *Talk About Writing: The Tutoring Strategies of Experienced Writing Center Tutors.* New York: Routledge.

Mandel, Ernest. 1975. *Late Capitalism.* London: New Left Books.

Mattison, Michael. 2011. *Centered: A Year in the Life of a Writing Center Director*. Raleigh, NC: Lulu.

Matzke, Aurora, Sherry Rankins-Robertson, and Bre Garrett. 2019. "'Nevertheless, She Persisted": Strategies to Counteract the Time, Place, and Structure for Academic Bullying of WPAs. In *Defining, Locating, and Addressing Bullying in the WPA Workplace*, edited by Cristyn Elder and Bethany Davila, 49-68. Logan: Utah State University Press.

Miley, Michelle. 2017. "Looking Up: Mapping Writing Center Work Through Institutional Ethnography." *Writing Center Journal* 36 (1): 103–29.

Monty, Randall. 2016. *The Writing Center as Cultural and Interdisciplinary Contact Zone*. New York: Palgrave/McMillan.

Morbidity and Mortality Weekly Report. 2001. "Pneumocystis Pneumonia—Los Angeles." Last updated May 5, 2001. https://www.cdc.gov/mmwr/preview/mmwrhtml/june_5.htm.

National Census of Writing. 2019. Accessed June 20, 2019. https://writingcensus.swarthmore.edu/.

National Alliance on Mental Illness. 2019. "LGBTQ." Last updated 2019. https://www.nami.org/find-support/lgbtq

Ocasio-Cortez, Alexandria. 2019. "In our house, we name a Queen of Hearts @NinaWest that is YOU! Thank you for being a relentless example of kindness, consciousness, compassion, and courage . . ." Twitter, May 11, 2019, 6:37 a.m. https://twitter.com/AOC/status/1127206100988833792.

Ozias, Moira, and Beth Godbee. 2011. "Organizing for Antiracism in Writing Centers: Principles for Enacting Social Change." In *Writing Centers and the New Racism: A Call for Sustainable Dialogue and Change*, edited by Laura Greenfield and Karen Rowan, 150–74. Logan: Utah State University Press.

Park, Madison. 2016. "Son's Last Texts Show His Fear As Killer Closes In." *CNN*, June 14, 2016. https://www.cnn.com/2016/06/13/us/eddie-justice-orlando-text-to-mom/index.html.

Pascoe, C. J. 2007. *Dude, You're a Fag: Masculinity and Sexuality in High School*. Berkeley: University of California Press.

Patterson, G. 2019. "Trans Research Ethics." Facebook, February 1, 2019.

Pauliny, Tara. 2011. "Queering the Institution: Politics and Power in the Assistant Professor Administrator Position." *Enculturation: A Journal of Rhetoric, Writing, and Culture* 10: 1–14.

Perryman-Clark, Staci, and Collin Lamott Craig, eds. 2019a. *Black Perspectives in Writing Program Administration: From the Margins to the Center*. Urbana, IL: Conference on College Composition and Communication/National Council of Teachers of English.

Perryman-Clark, Staci, and Collin Lamott Craig. 2019b. "Introduction: Black Matters: Writing Program Administration in Twenty-First Century Higher Education." In *Black Perspectives in Writing Program Administration: From the Margins to the Center*, edited by Staci Perryman-Clark and Collin Lamott Craig, 1–26. Urbana, IL: Conference on College Composition and Communication/National Council of Teachers of English.

Powell, Malea, Daisy Levy, Andrea Riley-Mukavetz, Marilee Brooks-Gillies, Maria Novotny, and Jennifer Fisch-Ferguson (The Cultural Rhetorics Theory Lab). 2014. "Our Story Begins Here: Constellating Cultural Rhetorics." *Enculturation: A Journal of Rhetoric, Writing, and Culture* 18. Last accessed August 15, 2019. http://enculturation.net/our-story-begins-here.

Pritchard, Eric Darnell. 2019. "Guest Blogger/Featured Scholar: 'When You Know Better, Do Better': Honoring Intellectual and Emotional Labor Through Diligent Accountability Practices." *Education, Liberation, and Black Radical Traditions: Carmen Kynard's Teaching and Reaching Site on Race, Writing and Classroom* (blog), July 8, 2019.

Restaino, Jessica. 2012. *First Semester: Graduate Students, Teaching Writing, and the Challenge of the Middle Ground*. Carbondale/Edwardsville: Southern Illinois Press.

Rhodes, Jacqueline. 2010. "Who Are We? What Do We Want To Become?" *WPA: Writing Program Administration* 33: 125–29.

Rhodes, Jacqueline, and Jonathan Alexander. 2019. "Queer(s in) Publics." Presentation at the Biennial Summer Institute of the Rhetoric Society of America, College Park, MD, 2019.

Riddick, Sarah, and Tristin Hooker, eds. 2019. "Special Issue: Race and the Writing Center." *Praxis: A Writing Center Journal* 16 (2). Last accessed June 20, 2019. http://www.praxisuwc.com/162-links-page.

Ridolfo, Jim. 2019. "Rhet Map: Mapping Rhetoric and Composition." Last modified September 20, 2019. http://rhetmap.org/.

Rihn, Andrew, and Jay D. Sloan. 2013. "Rainbows in the Past Were Gay: LGBTQIA in the WC." *Praxis: A Writing Center Journal* 10 (2): 1–13.

Rose, Joel. 2010. "Rutgers Student Remembered as Shy, Gifted Violinist." *National Public Radio*, October 1, 2010. https://www.npr.org/templates/story/story.php?storyId=130258242.

Rose, Rexford. 2016. "Queering the Writing Center: Shame, Attraction, and Gay Male Identity." Master's Thesis, East Carolina University.

Royster, Jacqueline Jones, and Gesa Kirsch. 2012. *Feminist Rhetorical Practices: New Horizons for Rhetoric, Composition, and Literacy Studies*. Carbondale: Southern Illinois University Press.

Ruti, Mari. 2017. *The Ethics of Opting Out: Queer Theory's Defiant Subjects*. New York: Columbia University Press.

Rylander, Jonathan J. 2017. "Complicated Conversations and Curricular Transgressions: Engaging Writing Centers, Studios, and Curriculum Theory." Doctoral Dissertation, Miami University of Ohio.

Sano-Franchini, Jennifer. 2016. " 'It's Like Writing Yourself into a Codependent Relationship with Someone Who Doesn't Even Want You!': Emotional Labor, Intimacy, and the Academic Job Market." *College Composition and Communication* 68 (1): 98–124.

Shipler, David K. 2004. *The Working Poor: Invisible in America*. New York: Vintage.

Simpkins, Neil, and Virginia Schwartz. 2015. "Queering RAD in Writing Center Studies." *Another Word from the Writing Center at the University of Wisconsin-Madison* (blog), November 9, 2015.

Sloan, Jay D. 1997. "Closet Consulting." *The Writing Lab Newsletter* 21 (10): 9–10.

Sloan, Jay D. 2003. "Centering Difference: Student Agency and the Limits of 'Comfortable' Collaboration." *Dialogue: A Journal for Writing Specialists* 8 (2): 63–74.

Sloan, Jay D. 2004. "Collaborating in the Contact Zone: A Writing Center Struggles with Multiculturalism." *Praxis: A Writing Center Journal* 1 (2): 8–10.

Sloan, Jay D. "Re: A Curious Silence and a Long-ish Response," WCenter Listserv, October 9, 2010. http://lyris.ttu.edu/read/messages?id=14813123#14813123.

Smith, Erec Steven. 2012. "Making Room for Fat Studies in Writing Center Theory and Practice." *Praxis: A Writing Center Journal* 10 (1): 17–23.

Strickland, Donna. 2011. *The Managerial Unconscious in the History of Composition Studies*. Urbana, IL: College Composition and Communication/National Council of Teachers of English.

Tarabochia, Sandra. 2016. "Investigating the Ontology of WAC/WID Relationships: A Gender-Based Analysis of Cross-Disciplinary Collaboration Among Faculty." *WAC Journal* 27: 52–73.

Tarabochia, Sandra. 2017. *Reframing the Relational: A Pedagogical Ethic for Cross-Curricular Literacy Work*. Urbana, IL: Conference on College Composition and Communication/National Council of Teachers of English.

Totenberg, Nina. 2020. "Supreme Court Delivers Major Victory to LGBTQ Employees." *National Public Radio*. June 15, 2020. https://www.npr.org/2020/06/15/863498848/supreme-court-delivers-major-victory-to-lgbtq-employees.

Tran, Ngọc Loan. 2013. "Calling IN: A Less Disposable Way of Holding Each Other Account-able," *BGD: Amplifying the Voices of Queer and Trans People* (blog), December 18, 2013. http://www.bgdblog.org/2013/12/calling-less-disposable-way-holding-accountable/.

Trump, Donald. 2017. ". . . Transgender individuals to serve in any capacity in the U.S. Military . . ." Twitter, July 26, 2017, 6:04 a.m. https://twitter.com/realDonaldTrump /status/890196164313833472.

Trump, Donald. 2019. "As we celebrate pride month . . ." Twitter, May 31, 2019, 12:12 p.m. https://twitter.com/realDonaldTrump/status/1134538166919204865.

Valles, Sarah Bancshbach, Rebecca Day Babcock, and Karen Keaton Jackson. 2017. "Writing Center Administrators and Diversity: A Survey." *The Peer Review: Journal for Writing Center Practitioners* 1. http://thepeerreview-iwca.org/issues/issue-1/writing-center -administrators-and-diversity-a-survey.

Wallace, David. 2002. "Out in the Academy: Heterosexism, Invisibility, and Double Consciousness." *College English* 65 (1): 53–66.

Warner, Michael. 1999. *The Trouble with Normal: Politics, Sex, and the Ethics of Queer Life.* Cambridge, MA: Harvard University Press.

Whitaker Manya. 2017. "The Unseen Labor of Mentoring." *ChronicleVitae*, June 12, 2017. https://chroniclevitae.com/news/1825-the-unseen-labor-of-mentoring.

White, Allen. 2004. "Reagan's AIDS Legacy/Silence Equals Death." *SFGate*, June 8, 2004. https://www.sfgate.com/opinion/openforum/article/Reagan-s-AIDS-Legacy-Silence -equals-death-2751030.php.

Wooten, Courtney Adams, Jacob Babb, and Brian Ray, eds. 2018. *WPAs in Transition: Navigating Educational Leadership Positions.* Logan: Utah State University Press.

World Health Organization. "Why The HIV Epidemic Is Not Over." Last updated 2019. https://www.who.int/hiv-aids/latest-news-and-events/why-the-hiv-epidemic-is-not-over.

The Writing Center Research Project. 2019. Last accessed June 20, 2019. https://owl .purdue.edu/research/writing_center_research_project/index.html.

Young, Vershawn Anthony. 2011. "Should Writers Use They Own English?" In *Writing Centers and the New Racism: A Call for Sustainable Dialogue and Change*, edited by Laura Greenfield and Karen Rowan, 61–72. Logan: Utah State University Press.

Yuhas, Alan. 2019. "Five Arrested in London Bus Attack on Two Lesbians." *The New York Times*, June 7, 2019. https://www.nytimes.com/2019/06/07/world/europe/lesbian -couple-london-bus-attack.html.

Zebroski, James. 2014. "'I Hate Straights': Talking with Students in a Gay and Lesbian Literature Course About the AIDS Crisis and Sex." Presentation given at the Annual Meeting of the University of Houston English Department Teaching Conference, Houston, TX, 2014.

INDEX

ABOUT THE AUTHOR

Travis Webster is assistant professor of writing and rhetoric at Virginia Tech University. He was the University of Houston–Clear Lake Writing Center Director from 2015 to 2018 and has worked in writing centers since 2002. His research appears in *College Composition and Communication, Writing Center Journal, WPA: Writing Program Administration,* and *The Peer Review.*